INTRODUCTION
The E-Type: British Motoring Masterpiece

There are many cars of the twentieth century that have claims to fame, of being icons of car design and driving, yet the number of true icons can almost be counted on one hand. Arguably the Jaguar E-Type leads the pack but there are other contenders: Porsche 911, Aston Martin DB4, Ferrari Daytona, Lamborghini Muira, Citroën DS, Willys Jeep, BMW 328 and Ford Mustang to name a few candidates.

There are other cars that their champions will cite as more worthy, not least from their national perspective: the Porsche 911 is of course a worldwide icon, but for many, the truth is that the Jaguar E-Type (or the XKE as it was tagged by Americans) was the global legend of its age. It was also a huge British design achievement on an international stage when British industrial design produced everything from cars such as the Mini and the Rover P6, to the QE2 liner, the Avro Vulcan, the Blackburn Buccaneer, the TSR2, the Vickers VC10 and then Concorde itself.

We must observe though that the Porsche 911 line continues to this day whereas E-Type does not. But that is not its fault, for that responsibility lies with what became British Leyland (BL) out of the British Motor Corporation (BMC) and merger with the Leyland Company in 1968; BLMC or just BL swallowed up Jaguar and several major British brands in league with British governments of all political hues whose hands ultimately lay upon the end of indigenous British volume car manufacturing. Latterly, Sir John Egan reinvented Jaguar from its darkest 'BL' days of declining quality and poor productivity in antiquated factories.

The E-Type was to become part of the BL process upon Jaguar, but has yet to be reincarnated despite several proposals and of course the F-Type as today's inheritor of the ethos.

We should not forget that, contrary to perceived wisdom, BL's famous Sir Michael Edwardes was not brought into BL by British Prime Minister Margaret Thatcher; he was in fact appointed in 1977 by a Labour leader named James Callaghan. It would be the 1980s before Jaguar threw off its yoke of 'State' thinking under BL. But Edwardes would free Jaguar to regain its brand identity. Yet all that was long after the heyday of Jaguar's 1950s Le Mans fame, the C-Type, D-Type and then the E-Type itself that was born as the 1960s began.

Revealed to a stunned world via a launch at the Salon d l'Auto de Genève in March 1961, the Jaguar E-Type (in fact to be badged as the E-Type Jaguar) actually caused the traffic to stop in several stylish cities when the inhabitants got their first sight of its incredible, yet never outrageous, style. This was no styling gimmick of a car, no marketing hype-led machine, no short-term fashion statement designed to shift metal. Instead, E-Type was a defining design that framed its own moment and its own sub-brand amid a new design language and a new era – the swinging Sixties. But E-Type would transcend even that decade's passing moments.

Incredibly, and best left behind in the darkest corner of design, was the attempt by designer Raymond Loewy (perhaps his ego) to improve or update the E-Type with his dandified restyling of the E-Type's front and rear. Yet today you can buy a scale model of it, if you must.

Aston Martin designer William Towns also produced a special-bodied V12 named as the Guyson E12.

E-Type brought new standards of speed, handling and style, all at a relative bargain price. Yet it did more than this, for its design language and driving experience defined a new age. Was it a revolutionary car design? Not quite, but it was a significant design and engineering advance of forensic engineering application, a car that was not

A red E-Type of late 1963 build shows off the amazing face of the Coventry cat. Those faired-in headlamps and bladed bumpers really were classic design items. (Photo Jaguar)

just the best of thinking, but fresh thought developed from a rapidly advancing, racing-led framework of ideas.

Was the convertible soft top or open roadster the defining E-Type? Some argue that the fastback coupé, or Fixed Head Coupé (FHC), was even more stylish and stunning, and it was revealed first too – at Geneva. Two camps existed but both E-Type variants were available from launch. Americans particularly loved the open-topped car.

Available new for a shade under £2,000, or half the price of a Ferrari, E-Type was of exquisite engineering and design sculpture yet one that was a paradox in being sold at a market price within reach of a larger part of society. A supercar, but not unobtainable – even if it remained a dream to the average working man amid a changing British society. Famous names from Billy Cotton, Innes Ireland, Briggs Cunningham, Max Aitken and many more owned early E-Types.

Much has been written about the E-Type Jaguar but this book attempts where possible, a fresh look at the design, development and, importantly, the modelling of the E-Type in an innovative new format that is also accessible and value for money. We do not have the space to supply every detail rivet by rivet, but we have taken a journey through the legend of the E-Type in factory, full-size metal, and die-cast and resin materials.

The last 1970s Series 3 E-Types were very different machines from the car's earlier marks, yet despite a slight corruption of the original styling and with the fitment of the supreme Jaguar V12 engine, the E-Type retained its character and allure in a new chapter of its life and marketing.

Few other cars can match the design and driving story of Jaguar's amazing E-Type – the true 150mph (almost!) British sports car that came in open convertible (roadster) and fixed-head (coupé) fastback types from launch. Some people think the original coupé type is prettier than the folding-roof open car, yet it is the open convertible that seems to get the glamour treatment from many.

Of that 150mph claim, well yes, it applied to factory test cars not least under the command of test driver and development engineer Norman Dewis, but as he stated to the author: 'The standard production-line cars did not really achieve 150mph. A good one, correctly set up might get to 147, but most struggled to beat 143mph. Coupés were easier aerodynamically, yet generated a bit of rear-end lift at high speed and they were heavier.'

Autocar proved a point with its famous road test in Belgium of an early E-type that did get to top the magical 150mph (nudging 152mph), but certain blueprinted tweaks had been made to the engine at the factory.

Yet the E-Type became a 150mph icon – despite the early cars having a slightly obstructive gearbox, a soon-to-be whining first gear, and a propensity for electrical maladies, rust and some rather cheap trim items. Did early E-Types look better than they went? So say many experts, yet some purists see beyond that. But the early brakes were weak and even the seats were soon to be improved – along with the gearbox. Purists might love a Series 1 (or S1) 3.8-litre 'flat-floor' early E-Type, but a later Series 2 4.2-litre drove faster and stopped better. But what of the best idea that was the 4.2-litre S1 – they did briefly exist.

For so long the second-tier E-Type under the pure ethos of the Series 1, the Series 2 (S2) may now be seen as the car that is better to drive and own. Either way, E-Type also rusted, as did so many other cars of its era.

The original E-Type looked a million dollars and was, according to Enzo Ferrari, the best-looking car in the world, yet it was produced on a relative shoestring of a budget by Sir William Lyons and his small team at Browns Lane, Coventry, and built in a factory of artisan skills and labour-intensive practices. Sir William was a major figure on the British and the international motor industry scene; although he was also known for his economies, he also managed to produce a British motoring masterpiece.

Buried inside the E-Type's design is more than engineering and styling; indeed, it was not so much styled as calculated in its body design by Malcolm Sayer whose talents were supreme yet lost to a nation and have never been adequately recognized.

Today an earlier car that is restored yet which retains some of its originality is worth a lot of money – nudging £200,000; rarer E-Types are worth a lot more. £500,000 might secure something very early and very special, and of course Low Drag and Lightweight E-Types have topped the million mark (more than US$7 million was achieved recently for a special car.

One aspect of the E-Type's design and development goes beyond the longevity of its appeal and its engineering and that is its reframing via updated engineering additions, into new E-Types of the type created and sold by the likes not just of Jaguar's own new Jaguar Classic brand (offering re-engineered, and continuation cars) itself, but also through the Eagle E-Type programme of new E-Types and the recreations and enhancements on offer across several specialist producers

of revised and enhanced E-Types in the modern era.

We might suggest that the Eagle E-Type range, with all its updates and improvements, offers what Jaguar might have offered if it had had the money, resources and opportunity to create a more bespoke, more tailored low-volume supercar – if that market had existed in the 1960s. Eagle really has reinvented the E-Type; the purist might have a view of such reinterpretation but the spirit of the E-Type, the Jaguar that remade and recast Jaguar, remains alive as a new car via Eagle.

Other purveyors of improved and restored and re-engineered E-Types today, include the famous Lynx, CKL, Winspeed and JD Classics offerings. Many specialists produce versions of rejuvenated or improved E-Types via restoration. A huge global business in Jaguar and

Below: Sir William Lyons, Jaguar's founder and guiding light, seen with a later, export-specification E-Type at his home, Wappenbury Hall – where he would work on his car designs and styling models. (Photo Jaguar)

Bottom: This December 1962 E-Type is an early 3.8-litre 'three-wiper' example in current use being driven as it was designed to be. Note the original features and fine-lined design elements all set off by that defining ellipsoid intake.

Below: Series 3 V12 coupé with a Bristol Britannia in the background. Note the E-Type changes of new front-end design, longer wheelbase and a taller, longer 2+2 coupé cabin turret. Also note the different, more aerodynamic windscreen shape and angle compared to earlier series.

Bottom: The E-Type coupé's rear aspect and small tailgate door and window designs are captured from a different viewpoint.

specific E-Type parts is served by the likes of the Martin Robey Company, SNG Barratt, RS Panels, Classic Motor Cars and the American Welsh Enterprises Inc. A company named Racing Green is also notable in Jaguar D-Type and E-Type history. Go to The Splined Hub for a really wonderful and forensic E-Type offering. The Classic Car Hub at Bibury also provides superb E-Types to drool over and even purchase.

Lynx (Lynx Motors) have produced recreations, or perhaps continuations, that include E-Type Lightweights, and five new examples of the original (Lindner-Nocker type) V-tailed E-Type Low Drag coupé. Examples of the earlier D-Type/XKSS have also been produced.

Jaguar itself via its Classic department now produces continuation E-Types of varying specifications including an electric EV version as Project Zero. In late 2017, Jaguar announced a modern revival of the 1968 E-Type S1½ roadster with an all-electric, zero-emission (at point of charge) propulsion system. This car has a 40kWh battery-powered electric motor and can accelerate to 60mph in 5.5 seconds. Sadly, the range is a mere 168 miles.

The famous 1960s Lightweight E-Types (of 110kg weight saving) saw twelve built of the eighteen planned examples with the remaining six allocated chassis numbers left unused. In 2015, Jaguar Land Rover's newly formed Special Operations division decided to build the remaining six cars to the original 1964 specification, to be sold as period competition vehicles suitable for historic motor sport – in which they now appear, driven by the new names of the sport.

In America, M. Marco Diez has recently completed the build of a re-imagined homage to the Low Drag coupé.

The Lyons line and Sayer's designs up to E-Type and XJ-13 have influenced later Jaguars into the modern design era. Shapes from Jaguar lead designers such as Lawson, Helfet, Callum and others have continued the foundations of the Lyons and Sayer 1950s/1960s design language. Peter Stevens's design for the 1990s Jaguar XJR-15 should not go uncited for its new ideas amalgamated into a legacy of styling clues that reeked of Jaguar and nothing else.

Of often-ignored note, the E-Type has proved to be an enduring favourite among modellers; the Jaguar Enthusiasts' Club even has its own modellers' section – which has kindly contributed to this book through Keith R. Powell as the club's model expert. From Amalgam to AUTOArt, Dinky and beyond, E-Type models across several scales and materials really are interesting. The Jaguar Daimler Heritage Trust is also an important part of preserving the E-Type and the Jaguar history and archive are accordingly acknowledged here. The E-Type Club is dedicated solely to the car and produces vital output, also being associated to Phillip Porter, the well-known Jaguar expert and writer.

This author feels, having been a Jaguar Lyons scholar and worked for and amid Jaguar, and having driven E-Type and the later XJ-S extensively, including in Africa and Australia, perhaps just a little qualified to offer a narrative and to create one that is not expensive nor elitist, and which delivers an accessible record of the car in full scale and in modelling scale. The diecast models of the E-Type have proved enduringly popular and have spawned an E-Type model movement.

Part of the CarCraft ethos is to offer modelling coverage alongside a narrative on the full-scale car. There are of course many E-Type books, but in this series, an accessible view from design to driving and modelling is presented. The story of Jaguar's leaping cat of an E-Type is well worth a fresh view.

Origins

Starting out as a back-street concern manufacturing motorcycle sidecars, the company that became Jaguar rose to become a global brand and the definition of British sporting and cars prowess. Few manufacturers can cite a product line that includes grand sporting saloons such as SS 100, Mk V, Mk VII, Mk X, XK120-140-150, the C-Type, D-Type, the vital E-Type Mk 1/Mk 2, XJ6, XJ13 and the more recent Jaguars.

The truth is that one key personality created this massive company that today, despite modern issues in the auto industry, remains a golden brand, a national gem. Sir William Lyons (1901–85) was Jaguar and he even shaped his own cars into the Lyons line. He really was an amazing character and a national hero. Lyons was of Irish paternal lineage and Blackpool was where he grew up. With an early interest in engineering, he was apprenticed to the Crossley Motors Company.

We should not forget Williams Lyons' initial business partner William Walmsley, who, although he sold out his share of the nascent company and moved on, also had a talent for body design and coachbuilding and went on to design a very early aerodynamic, aerofoil-shaped caravan – decades before they became popular.

Jaguar was to be brand-born from the Swallow outfit, from inauspicious and somewhat ordinary beginnings yet rising to global fame and enduring iconography. From 1922, its early days in Cocker Street,

Blackpool (not Coventry), Swallow Sidecar, which was to be officially registered as the Swallow Sidecar Coachbuilding Company, began coachbuilding and small-scale manufacturing of sidecar bodies and by 1927 had produced a small car with a unique, sporting body fabricated over an Austin chassis and engine. A small but very stylish open body (with a removable roof) was grafted by Lyons onto the base Austin Seven unit. Here was William Lyons' first car. But Blackpool was isolated from the crucible of the British engineering heartland of the Midlands, so Lyons and his business moved to Foleshill, Coventry, in 1928 to be closer to the action and their suppliers.

By late 1930, Lyons had created a very smart little Swallow Seven two-door car of a new style that looked expensive but was actually a smaller, cheaper car. The interior was leather-lined with a padded cocoon that added a certain luxuriousness to the humble Austin base unit. The styling was of streamliner look and a glossy chrome radiator shell topped off the quality effect. Here lay Lyons' early marketing ethos. Yet underneath lay an Austin. Soon, Lyons was adding bodies to other makes of cars supplied as running chassis – as European coachbuilders – Carrosserie and Karossen – were also doing.

In 1931, Lyons then decided to build a more upmarket two-seater open sports car which was stunning in its style and sculpture even if it did rely upon a

Mid-1930s SS100 – the precursor to the Jaguar formula seen in the E-Type. The Lyons line began at this time.

The first iteration of the SS Jaguar saloon ethos captured in early 1930s styling and fashion. (Photo Jaguar)

proprietary engine sourced from another carmaker – the Standard Company. Through prior and later respective agreements with Austin, Standard, Wolseley, Henleys the car dealers and other companies, Lyons then organized the creation of a car to be sold under its own name of SS, or S/S as some cited it. A Standard-Swallow was briefly mentioned prior to the SS branding taking dominance. Lyons would use a Standard-supplied engine for some years.

The grand and elegant SS 1 series was born and from 1933 to 1935 evolved from the SS 1 two-door coupé-type into a two-door saloon and an open four-seater convertible, all as SS or SS-branded cars. The chassis were built for SS by Rubery-Owen and the engines, of 16hp and 20hp, came via Lyons' arrangement with Standard. Gradually, Lyons was defining his own engineering parameters as well as setting a body style innovation. By 1936, Lyons had built over 7,500 cars since starting in Blackpool.

Even though Ford were producing a side-valve V8 engine, Lyons, by 1934, via the advice of engineer and tuner Harry Weslake, decided to create an overhead valve-type engine to replace the old Standard-derived designs in his cars. By 1936, William M. Heynes had started in Lyons' employ and became an essential part of the Lyons legend.

So, the Swallow Sidecar Company officially became the S.S. Car Company Ltd. As early as 1934, the company exported its first SS cars to the United States. In late 1935, the S.S. Company produced a new model with the name of Jaguar. This car was a large 2.5-litre car with the new overhead valve cylinder head-type of much greater efficiency and had more power and torque.

S.S. had stood for Swallow Sidecar, or was it Swallow Special? This was the SS-branded car reflecting the Swallow Sidecar's original name, yet sadly to be mistakenly contaminated in some minds by terminology stemming from the Nazis.

So, the S.S. Company was named Jaguar in 1945 in a new post-war world where SS was unacceptable and Lyons began to build himself a major new marque. Jaguar was a name previously used by Armstrong Siddeley for one of its aero-engines and Lyons liked it and its associations, so he gained permission to use it as the name of his new marque.

Before that happened, back in the 1930s had come the SS 90 and the defining SS 100 as open convertible two-seater sporting cars of great style with the Standard-derived straight-six engine of over 2.0 litres' capacity. Many feel that this is where the true Jaguar ethos was born, if not in name but in concept that would run to the E-Type (and beyond). The long-bonnet, flowing styling and use of curves set a Jaguar hallmark that Lyons defined and latterly, his post-1950 designer Malcolm Sayer evolved and reframed.

Low numbers of the SS 90 were built with twenty-three constructed. But the car was then turned into the more potent SS 100 with 2.5 litres, then 3.5 litres and benefitting from Lyons' saloon car developments and his revised engine design of 1935. The SS 100 became big news and a new chapter for the S.S. Company; the car was the first true thoroughbred of the Lyons line. With power, grace, revised suspension and expensive engineering thrown at it, SS 100 from 1936 to 1939 became a much-desired 100hp, 100mph, upmarket sporting roadster machine that made Lyons and his brand. The car cost just over £400 on launch and was value for money even in an age when a small house cost not a lot more. The SS 100 also entered motor sport and by the outbreak of the Second World War really had carved a niche for Lyons and his nascent brand.

After a wartime interregnum, Lyons was soon to make an even bigger mark on British motoring.

By 1948, Jaguar had produced the stopgap Mk V saloon with its pre-war ingredients refreshed until a better supply of materials allowed totally new cars to be

built once the shadow of wartime austerity had lifted by 1950. This was also the last pushrod-type (Standard-derived) engine in a Jaguar and was essentially a restyle and refresh of the pre-war saloon. A few coupé versions of the Mk V were also manufactured. Just over 10,000 Mk V were built, but by 1951 Jaguar had readied its defining new Mk VII sporting saloon. From then on Jaguar never really looked back and Le Mans and sports car production beckoned.

Lack of an in-house engine had in the mid-1930s led Lyons, Heynes and the engineering team to create their own modified overhead-valve engine, but then they went the whole hog and designed their own, entirely new complete engine in the form of the superb high-performance twin-overhead camshaft XK series of 1948. This cost money and Lyons was taking a huge gamble with his finances and his future. Yet within a decade he would be knighted for his efforts.

This engine remained in production in modified form until the early 1990s. It had powered the XK120/140/150 series of the 1950s, the C- and D-Types, the early E-Types and a range of saloons – saloons being a core element of Jaguar, yet often overshadowed in some arenas by the sports cars and their racing legends. Jaguar's first true defining grand sporting saloon was the 1951-launched, XK-powered Jaguar Mk VII series, a stylish grand tourer with handling and performance decades before BMW created its own incarnations of such a formula.

The XK engine had really been created for use in such a Jaguar saloon – Jaguar's money earner and export sales success. But fitted in the XK series of 120, 140, and the slightly fatter 150, Jaguar laid down the cars that were the foundations of the C-Type that led to the D-Type and the outcome that was the E-Type.

William 'Bill' Heynes, Walter Hassan and Claude Baily (SS Cars' chief designer and ex-Morris Motors) had defined the straight-six engine in terms of power, torque and smooth operation. Other manufacturers would race to catch up as from 1948 the new engine debuted in the new line of Jaguar's focus – the XK120.

Prototypes

Lyons produced a series of prototypes and one-off concept-car design studies that he styled himself. Perhaps his most famous such stepping-stone design idea was the 1938 pre-war Jaguar 100 coupé that he built a single example of. With its rather Bugatti-esque cabin turret to its rear wheel spats and curvaceous themes, it was a pointer towards the 1950s XK series. In 1946 Lyons created an XL design-concept prototype which was clearly a precursor to the 1948 design for the XK120. By late 1949, he had thought of developing the XK120; the arrival of Malcolm Sayer at his behest gave rise to an XK120-based aerodynamics study prototype known as the XK120 C – effectively the C-Type. Next came a C/D concept or XKC2; also known as the light alloy, it was a precursor to Sayer's D-Type and the E-Type design language and saw the first deployment of an elliptical form and elliptical front air intake.

William Lyons tried his hand at an aerodynamic racer of pontoon-body style with a smooth, slab-sided look, but that was a one-off. But it was the light alloy C/D/XKC2 concept that was the true design step-change that would lead to another prototype – the E1A (of 3.0 litres). It was the E1A (of chassis and alloy tub-type design) that truly became the E-Type semi-monocoque design and it was reached via the XK series and Le Mans success, as the E2A development car.

1950s Flyers

Jaguar's first true post-war sporting roadster was the XK120: here was a 3,442cc straight-six two-door sports car of soft-top open type (from 1952 a fixed hardtop) with styling that took British upmarket motoring to a new level. The XK engine had hemispherical combustion

XK120 to XK140 defined the two-seater sporting Jaguar design. This car captured every element of Lyons' ideas and talent for creating something unique in style and speed.

Below: Stirling Moss and Norman Dewis in the XK003 C-Type at the 1952 Mille Miglia. They skidded off and damaged the car. Dewis repaired it on the road but they were out of the race pace. (Photo Jaguar)

Bottom: C-Type was Sayer's evolution of the early XK series for racing purposes – specifically Le Mans. Here began the aero design of Jaguar legend.

chamber design, an inclined head, highly efficient valve, camshaft and crankshaft functions allied to a twin overhead-valve configuration. The engine functioned at new heights of efficiency and output, but it was a touch narrow in its top-end design, said some engineers.

Early XK120s were effectively hand built and constructed in aluminium alloy. As such, the production costs were high and after a reputed 240 had been fabricated, Lyons had by 1951 created a new pressed-panel production line-built bodyshell for the XK120. The car was cheaper to make, and a massive sales hit, notably in America and the Commonwealth. So too was the then concurrent Jaguar Mk V saloon with which the XK120 shared a (shortened) chassis.

XK120 was a top seller for Jaguar with over 12,000 sales. The forthcoming XK140 derivative and the bigger XK150 would both also achieve sales of around 10,000 units. Jaguar made money in the 1950s

and used some of it to develop its racing cars, notably the C-Type and D-Type.

From 1954 there followed the XK140 range as an updated XK120. XK140 had the new rack and pinion steering, disc brakes, and revised specifications amid styling revisions. A more heavily revised XK150 arrived in 1957, still with the same XK engine (latterly 3.8 litre), and with revised external body panels draped over the pre-existing XK140 toolings. An S version had triple carburettors and sports trims. Often overlooked is that this XK150 also created a 2+2 variant in a sporting Jaguar – before E-Type latterly did the same thing. A two-seater open roadster XK150 was also produced.

As the 1950s progressed, Jaguar went racing, and the XK cars provided the basis of the C-Type as an initial step. It was this car that debuted and tested the all-round disc brakes set-up that was a Jaguar innovation (long after Sir Frederick Lanchester had designed such a mechanism). Major international motor-sport events, notably Le Mans, saw developed Jaguars, leading to the D-Type, make a massive mark upon the sport in the Jaguar Works team and private teams such as the Ecurie Ecosse.

Italian designers took the XK120 and XK140 basis to create several specials or design-concept cars on Jaguar themes; the XK120 Supersonic by Carrozzeria Ghia of Turin cannot be left uncited in the annals of Jaguar design en route to the E-Type. Some observers feel that Jaguar's own Malcolm Sayer was not uninfluenced by the Disco Volanti as a design of an Italian styling special. All this took place in the early era of the XK series, prior to D-Type into E-Type via Coventry not Turin or Milan.

C-Type and the Dawn of Design

Lyons had seen the XK120 perform well at Le Mans in 1950, but could Jaguar do better? The resulting development that was the C-Type gained a first-try victory at Le Mans as early as 1951 and won again in 1953 (1952 had seen aerodynamic and mechanical experimentation tried out on the cars and they had overheated). The C-Type's body had been lightened and taken from chassis/girder design to spaceframe and panel-work type.

Jaguar's new designer and aerodynamics expert Malcolm Sayer, fresh in with aviation and elliptical calculus knowledge, smoothed over the XK120 and made the C-Type much more slippery. Sayer had expert (aviation-derived) knowledge of engines and internal as well as external airflow. He ducted air into the C-Type's engine bay, into the carburettors and onto the brakes. 1952's Le Mans errors were soon forgotten.

Homologation rules required fifty such cars to be built and available for public sale, and so were born the rare road-going C-Types. An even lighter, later production batch also saw such cars race with the new Dunlop disc brakes. 1953 saw these C-Types dominate Le Mans with Tony Rolt and Duncan Hamilton driving to victory.

F.R. 'Lofty' England was Jaguar's development engineering figure and Walter Hassan was Jaguar's engine design expert, William Heynes was Jaguar's engineering leader who had joined Lyons in 1935, with a later focus on chassis development, Robert Knight was drivetrain engineer, Claude Baily an engineer, Cyril Holland the bodybuilder, William Rankin the design modeller, Robert Blake the prototype build expert, and Norman Dewis a development engineer and driver of famed testing and assessment abilities.

Malcolm Sayer would join the team as designer and aerodynamicist and rise to fame in the 1950s. As Jaguar's post-1950 body designer, he should be rightly credited with creating defining forms for the marque, yet we should attribute the Lyons line as Sir William's own creation of an early form of car-design language. He guided design sketches and clay model development and had such clay and wooden proposals in part-scale and full size brought to his home at Wappenbury Hall where he made modifications to the body styles until he was satisfied with the look. Of note, the 1968-launched Jaguar XJ-6 body shape was principally of his design (with some Sayer input). XJ-6 was a cohesive, organic form that was perfect from every angle and at every junction of panel.

So the important step that was the C-Type was an XK120 derivative of 1951 (with production-scale models in 1952), with a revised aerodynamic body and soon-to-be-innovated H. Butler/J. Wright-patented function disc brakes (Dunlop-Jaguar developed) – which in this application suffered from overheating, perhaps due to the more-enveloping aerodynamics front bodywork.

Fifty C-Types and subsequently fifty D-Types were required to be built to adhere to homologation rules

Above: Norman Dewis, Jaguar test driver and development engineer. From brakes to transmission to suspension and aerodynamic testing, he was the man. (Photo Jaguar)

Left: Dewis the man, captured at the famous Jabbeke high-speed test in October 1953, about to take XK120, registered MDU 524 (with aerodynamic canopy fitted) to 172mph.

D-Type, the revolutionary elliptical device of Sayer's mind and Jaguar's engineering. Short-nose, long-nose, finned or not, it went like the wind. (Photo Jaguar)

D-Type

Then arrived the short-nose and long-nose iterations of Sayer's elliptically shaped and alloy-bodied homage to the mix of wings and wheels that was the 172-mph D-Type. In D-Type Sayer brought together everything he had learned about airflow, elliptical co-ordinates, surface effects, area-rule and mathematical techniques to manage effects known as skewness and kurtosis, and lift and drag reduction, in order to shape a world-class automotive sculpture that also happened to become a Le Mans-winning racing car for 1955 (driven by Mike Hawthorn and Ivor Bueb), and with the Ecurie Ecosse D-Type (driven by Ninian Sanderson and Ron Flockhart) winning in 1956.

This team triumphed again the following year with unwritten Jaguar support – Jaguar having removed itself from competition. D-Types, with and without rear stabilizing fins for very-high-speed driving, became a benchmark and Jaguar reached international legend status with five Le Mans wins and top-tier placings at Le Mans, Silverstone, Spa and many other tracks, and even sold homologated D-types

and the D-Type XKSS variants, to great acclaim.

One D-Type, the seventh production car (484 UXC), was ordered new for delivery to Australia in 1955 by privateer William 'Bill' Stillwell. It was latterly owned and campaigned by Frank Gardner and Porsche racer Richard Attwood – he being a 1970s Le Mans winner.

As for making fifty D-Types, were sixty-seven built? Were forty-two or forty-three non-race versions actually built? Significantly, these were production-type cars sold to private customers and road-going use was not impossible for these cars. But at least twenty-five of these cars were unsold. The answer was to modify them into something more saleable – the road-going XKSS derivative with a proper, weather-protective windscreen and frame, a few cabin comforts and the fitment of bumpers.

Built until 1957 with eighteen team cars and a reputed fifty-three customer cars as well as sixteen unsold chassis converted to XKSS specification, D-Type laid all the foundations for its successor as a road-going car – the E-Type. D-Type even

In this – a more modern iteration of a D-Type, as a recreation based on a 1971 E-Type – the sheer genius of Sayer's scaling and mathematical shaping is captured. It was but one step from D-Type to E-Type in design-language terms in 1959.

contributed some pressings and parts to the E-Type's structural design.

In 2018 Jaguar announced its new D-Type recreation or continuation project whereby a newly built 1955/56-specification D-Type with XK 3.4-litre twin-cam engine could be purchased after build by the Jaguar Classic division. Twenty-five were to be built.

Newly knighted Sir William Lyons had not forgotten his sporting saloons either and came up with the XK-powered (2.4-litre and then 3.4-litre) Mk 1 saloon in 1957. This was the first Jaguar full-monocoque production-car body design and as a sporting saloon was the car that would evolve into the more famous revised design of the slim-pillared Mk 2 of 1960s fame with a certain unwanted notoriety among the criminal fraternity as a getaway car. The car's classic status would later be secured by a certain fictional television detective by the name of Morse.

But it was the defining D-Type that was the stiffest, fastest, strongest racing car monocoque and 'tub' of the 1950s: D-Type was revolutionary in aerodynamic and in structural terms. It also took the disc-braked C-Type to a new, definitive form and function.

Norman Dewis was instrumental in the testing of the D-Type, as he would be for E-Type. Indeed, Dewis would work closely with Jaguar aerodynamicist and body designer Malcolm Sayer. The pair would experiment with cooling, drag-reduction and lift-reduction variations to the D-Type – experimenting by hand, tuft-test and measurements in artisan fashion in-the-metal. What they learned on D-Type they applied to E-Type. 1950s Jaguar mechanic Ron Gaudion was a key figure in the Le Mans developments which included the use of quick-change brake calipers on long-nose D-Types. Brian J. Martin was a long-serving Jaguar development engineer who worked on E-Type development.

As early as 1954 the D-Type was ready to race at Silverstone's International Trophy Meeting, but Jaguar withdrew the cars in order to concentrate on preparing for Le Mans.

Jaguar competed at the Vingt Quatre Heures Grand Prix d'Endurance – the 24-hour endurance race – at Le Mans from 1951 to great effect. Stirling Moss was unlucky not to have a debut D-Type victor in 1954; Duncan Hamilton in a D-Type came second. A young Mike Hawthorn would win his and D-Type's first Le Mans the following year in 1955. In 1956, two D-Types would crash at Le Mans. The Scottish racing team Ecurie Ecosse won the 1956 Le Mans with a D-Type. In 1957 the Jaguar D-Type took not just victory – at the hands of Ecurie Ecosse – but all three top places on the podium. Ecurie Ecosse D-Types were first and second (as cars XKD 606 and XKD 603 respectively) and a separate Jaguar Works D-Type (XKD

5013) third. Other D-Types came in fifth and sixth.

D-Type was built as short-nosed and long-nosed variants and through Jaguar and the Ecurie Ecosse team stamped a mark on the world motor-sport stage. No less a figure than Jim Clark raced a D-Type. Of note, it was in a short-nosed D-Type painted creamy white (XKD517) that Clark created lap times for a British circuit of over 100mph for the first time. The Murkett brothers owned XKD 517 and then Border Reivers. Duncan Hamilton raced a D-Type alongside various drivers including Archie Scott Brown and Henry Taylor. The Border Reivers team ran the Clark D-Type in 1958 and won twelve races out of a calendar of twenty events.

Perhaps one of the D-Types' most intriguing motor-sport moments was its competing in the 1956 Dakar Grand Prix in Senegal where D-Type XKD 150 came fifth in the hands of Graham Whitehead. Sadly, this was the car that when sold on to Duncan Hamilton, and then driven by Tony Dennis, fatally crashed at the Goodwood Easter Meeting less than a month after its African appearance. The wrecked car was rebuilt only to crash fatally again in an Asian race in the 1960s, yet was rebuilt again and exists today

XKSS

From the race-going and occasionally road-going D-Type came a softer version as the solely road-going derivative known as the XKSS. In 1957 Jaguar created a D-Type derivative. The Company suffered an infamous fire at the factory in Browns Lane in early 1957 and concentrated on actually making cars rather than racing them. It was at this time that the E-Type evolved from the 1950s process of pace and of production design. From the D-Type, the next design-derivative iteration and alphabetical follow-on was of course E-Type. En route was the XKSS as part of the process – an in-between car after D-Type and before E-Type.

Mechanically identical to the D-Type, for the 149mph XKSS minor structural

The XK150 was wider than the XK120 and its XK140 derivative. Here, in the XK150 we see the first iteration of the larger Jaguar sportster. The E-Type was next – after the input of the D-Type's more overtly racingng genes. In XK150, Jaguar tapped into a growing customer base, notably in America.

The amazing shape of D-Type transcribed to road going car for sale to the private buyer. Adding a windscreen, passenger seat and weather kit did not detract from the ethos. Twelve were built, several more are cited, and today you can buy a new one from Jaguar – or you could. (Photos Jaguar)

changes were restricted to removing the dividing brace panel between the driver's cockpit and the left-hand spare seat and the addition of a passenger door. A full set of instruments, a basic – very basic – roof or hood, a rear boot/trunk lid luggage carrier – all were fitted. The very slim, blade-like bumpers were true precursors to the E-Type's bumpers.

It is suggested that Duncan Hamilton (D-Type racer) had converted his own D-Type into a revised, one-off road-going variant similar to the XKSS, but others closer to Jaguar suggest that the XKSS was a factory derivation designed to appeal to Americans and to American production-sports-car racing series and the rules required to enter them. The famous American racer Briggs Cunningham also happened to be Jaguar's New York State agent and had a hand in XKSS, as did Robert Blake who built experimental and racing car bodies for Cunningham. Blake would be deployed to Jaguar in England to help create the limited production run of XKSS cars.

Twelve initial XKSSs were built – on D-Type chassis numbers. Four more are cited. Sixteen early XKSSs were individually converted D-Types. Of note, the XKSS had a D-Type chassis number as well as an XKSS non-sequential chassis number nomenclature. The fire at the Jaguar factory is said to have destroyed the toolings and panels and production ceased – except that at least two later D-Type-to-XKSS conversions are reputed to be in the Jaguar archives.

The XKSS limited-series production cars were sold worldwide in the late 1950s and became instant collectors' items. Today a real one is worth millions and the more recently built official Jaguar Classic Works continuation is not far behind.

From Spitfire to D-Type?

Of interest, XKSS and D-Type were elliptically shaped and had elliptically formed structural members – the ellipse beneficially dealing with aerodynamics and also aiding stress and torsional force absorption in metal respectively. As such, the D-Type was aerodynamically and structurally similar to the techniques taken in the design of the earlier 1930s Supermarine Spitfire aircraft – a device not without some small links to Jaguar's designer, ex-Bristol Company and aviation engineer Malcolm Sayer and his own knowledge of elliptical and mathematical design processes involving axes, co-ordinates, plotting and logarithms. This aspect of Sayer's work and, of note, the E-Type's body design and styling process and realization in the metal, is rarely cited in accounts about Jaguar or the E-Type.

From this mathematical process came the E-Type EA prototypes E1A and the more structurally advanced E2A and then its production series that marked the beginning of a new decade. E-Type was a Lyons-led idea for a mass-production reinterpretation of the D-Type. With his marketing and money head on, Lyons knew that volume sales of a road-going car, with the allure and a percentage of the D-Type's handling and performance, would make money. It is unlikely that he envisaged just how famous it would be.

Of interest, the E2A or EA2 prototype was retained under the ownership of a Jaguar employee for many decades and is now a famous car appearing at car shows.

As the 1950s ended, Jaguar was a on a high, and despite certain unfortunate events including the fire at the Coventry factory, it was about to come up with a further act of genius, one very obviously to be called the E-Type.

The last of the XK150 series at speed up against the Jaguar Mk 1 saloon – subjected to Coombs modifications if you please. Both these cars predate E-Type. (Photo Jaguar)

The Jaguar racing legend captured with a Lightweight E-Type surrounded by some its antecedents in their competition specifications. (Photo Jaguar)

The amazing XJ13 came along in the mid-1960s as an incredible amalgam of D-Type, E-Type and other Sayer ingredients. Naturally it was tested by Mr Dewis. A stunning piece of Jaguar design and one that, sadly, did not become a volume production special. If it had, it would have certainly seen off Ferrari, Lamborghini and Porsche.

Coupé (rear) and later roadster or fixed head convertible (FHC) (foreground) display the design differences between the two types and their evolving designs – such as the headlamp treatment.

Design & Detail

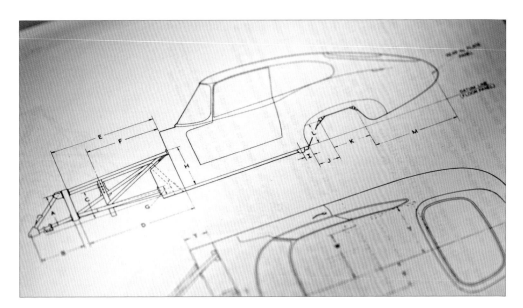

Drawing of E-Type showing the monocoque-type main body allied to a front end of triangulated spaceframe-type support sub-chassis, over which was draped the one-piece bonnet pressing. (Photo Jaguar)

We can see that it is proven that the E-Type took its basis from previous Jaguar practice and development across its prototypes, road cars and the Le Mans cars. This process included the innovative use of disc-brakes, and the early application of aerodynamics research to a mass-production British car (for example, beyond the production volume of Bristol Cars). Apart from Frank Costin and few specialists, aerodynamics was not a theme given much consideration in the late 1950s, unless of course you were Bristol, Citroën or Saab or Porsche, or more obscurely, Jowett of Bradford, Yorkshire. The 'Coventry Cats', of Jaguar fame, advanced the art of road-car aerodynamics and Sayer was the high priest of such scientific arts.

It was Jaguar's learning from its experiences with the XK120, 140, 150 series, C-Type and D-Type, notably in motorsport competition, that paved the way for the E-Type's success. Robert 'Bob' Knight was a key figure in the engineering of the E-Type, notably in the chassis, drivetrain and suspension. He championed the reduction of noise, vibration and harshness allied to handling prowess. Jaguar spent nearly five years developing and honing the E-Type's new suspension and its handling. Unlike today's multibillion-pound design and development costings, Lyons and his Jaguar concern, created E-Type on a budget and with a core team of less than twenty-five people, all of them road- and race-proven in thinking and experience.

The first E-Type prototype, known as EA or E1A, was interesting in that the bonnet design was different from the final production tooling: it was not a total clamshell type down to the sill, but only extended in its horizontal side alignment to halfway down the wing line. EA was wider too, but its DNA was obvious,

As follows, the E-Type's advance can be defined into separate engineering and design areas

Body Design and Structure

In E-Type we see a car that looks like its name, or has a clear feel of intent. The body shape is taught yet timeless, a touch feline or esoteric in a prehensile manner. The long bonnet, the curved front wing shoulders and the suggestion of powerful hindquarters all remind us of a wild animal about to pounce – a jaguar perhaps?

Here was styling that was not – for the designer was not a stylist but a design engineer with artistic skills which he translated via mathematical practices. From any angle, E-Type works and remains one of the greatest pieces of industrial design ever to come out of Great Britain.

The car had haunches, an expensive-to-manufacture curved windscreen and very clever details to control airflow. Sayer originally wanted an even more curved windscreen with smoother transition to the sides of the car, and in the later E-Type revisions of 2+2 coupé body and S3 design, this was achieved.

E-Type was a monocoque body-type car, yet it also deployed a triangulated frame-on front engine and suspension mounting system. So, it was in part a monocoque-hybrid type. It weighed just 2,900lb (1,318kg).

The main bodyshell of floorpan, undertray, sills, bulkhead and rear end were welded, pressed steel toolings built up to form a bodyshell 'tub' section that formed the main centre-body. However, a very large, one-piece bonnet panel encompassed the entire front end of the car, underneath which could be found a sub-chassis of an engine support cradle built largely of square section steel beams (often erroneously cited as tubes) that also carried the suspension and steering. D-Type had used expensive magnesium alloy to save weight, but at great cost to purchase: E-Type would use steel and a touch of aluminium. Yet E-Type was about 500lb lighter than a hefty old XK150 and its chassis, so was faster even if it used a similar engine.

E-Type featured very strong sills to each side of the monocoque floorpan 'punt'; the sills were wide and strong, yet in truth, the steel spaceframe beams of the engine bay that were mounted onto the main front bulkhead and front of the sills were stronger and stiffer – in order to carry the engine and its torque loads and contain the suspension – than the sill panels themselves. This meant that in a heavy accident, the sills were compressed by the lack of deformation in the engine-to-bulkhead spaceframe framework mounted ahead of them and onto their front end. Ultimately, the sills would bend under

load near their midpoint and allow the less-deformed frontal spaceframe area to intrude backwards. Reinforcing the floor wells with thick steel plate was not uncommon in older E-Types and improved the stiffness of the sills and cabin area. Little known beyond Jaguar experts is the fact that the E-Type also utilized D-Type sill toolings and front bulkhead pressings.

The front-opening bonnet was like any car fitted with such, vulnerable to the mounting hinges corroding. If they were left to rot, it meant that in a frontal impact, the bonnet would simply fly off and push back over or through the windscreen, risking decapitating the occupants with the sharp trailing edge of the bonnet. Even safety-conscious Saab had to work out a way to prevent this with its own front-hinged bonnets. Triumph was also similarly troubled by such design issues. Jaguar worked hard on the bonnet system to reduce this threat. Changes were also made to the bonnet locking system in early production.

Today it is vital that this under-bonnet spaceframe remains rust-free in order to retain torsional stiffness at the front of the car. Body restorations can easily run to many thousands of pounds, or dollars.

The E-Type design was neither unsafe, nor badly designed, it was simply of its era in research and knowledge terms. The long nose offered good impact energy absorption in a crash. Rollover protection was, like nearly all cars of the 1960s, not a significant design factor. A low centre of gravity and a resistance to roll dynamics was an E-Type benefit.

Sayer's Style

'Styled by Malcolm Sayer' is a phrase that many use of the E-Type. But the fact was that Sayer was an engineer, a designer and not a stylist in the traditional sense of fashion and form. He had an interesting duality of mathematical, engineering training and brain function, yet also an artistic and musical side to his thinking and creativity. This was highly unusual in 1950s Britain. Of a different personality

Below: Sir William Lyons stands beside the launch E-Type coupé and its perfect form. Note the external bonnet latch.

Bottom: The very rare E-Type prototype E2A contained many design elements that crossed over from D-Type racer to E-Type road-going sports car. Note the rear fin. (Photo Jaguar)

to the more conservative Lyons, the pair did however work closely together. Lyons' father had been musical so perhaps there was an empathy amid the engineering.

Malcolm G. Sayer (1916–70) did sculpt and shape the E-Type into is amazing form, but he also used mathematical processes and aerodynamics calculations to achieve the car's shape. He calculated the curves, compound curves, ratios and panel shapes of the E-Type using mathematics and its techniques. The under-curve of the lower side panels, the angle of the fast back, the shape of the windscreen, the relationship of length to width to height – all were the result of calculation, plots, co-ordinates and science, not solely of flamboyant artistic expression.

He plotted his shapes and multi-dimensional forms using advanced mathematics, logarithms and elliptical axis calculations and focused on aerodynamic surface development. The more efficient aerodynamics of the ellipse, first investigated and proven by British design innovator Sir Frederick Lanchester in the 1890s, and latterly by German aerodynamics experts, were of great interest to Sayer. Of note, the Jaguar Company would absorb both Daimler and Lanchester.

Sayer hated the idea of needing to add a wing or spoiler or lip or a moveable aerodynamic device to a car body in order to make it aerodynamically correct; instead he tried to avoid such 'stick-on' solutions by making the shape correct and aero-efficient in the first place. Despite some aerodynamic lift at very high speed, E-Type reduced the spectre of such aerodynamic instability and did not need any production car spoilers. However, racing developments for cars likely to travel at high velocity (such as at Le Mans) did see dive-planes, fences and small wing panels added on a somewhat experimental basis.

Sayer had trained at Loughborough College. His first engineering job was at the famous aircraft maker, the Bristol Company, from September 1938. He rose fast and invented a new way of cooling

The smiling 'cat': original E-Type shows off its finessed and delicate design elements at launch. Note the front intake and chrome stripe design motif. (Photo Jaguar)

aircraft engines by using reversal-effect airflow, as used in the engine installations of the Bristol Blenheim and Beaufighter. He also designed and co-built the Gordano, a late-1940s two-seater sports car as a private venture with two other men – Messrs Fry and Cesar. Sayer managed to incorporated some aspects of his aerodynamic thinking into the little sportster, particularly with a horizontally mounted rear spare wheel to act as an airflow trigger, but was limited in his effect by the car's basic design intent as a cheap roadster special.

The Bristol Company would soon produce its own BMW–derived first car, then its own highly aerodynamic cars designed by Messrs Hobbs and Lane and developed in the company's own wind tunnel (latterly to see Mr Sevier as chief engineer of Bristol Cars). Sayer had left Bristol by this time, and after a trip abroad, emerged into the employ of Sir William Lyons at Jaguar as the 1950s dawned – more by accident than design.

William Lyons hired Sayer personally and then handed the young engineer over to 'Lofty' England and Bill Heynes for development. Sayer's first task was to make Jaguar's XK120-derived C-Type into a slippery Le Mans racer. Then, as we

This May 1962 coupé is of pure lines and sublime design. Faired-in lamps, low cabin fastback turret, metallic steel-grey paint, dark red leather and non-standard wheels all add to the classic coupé in a perfection of form like no other. No wonder Enzo Ferrari said this was the most beautiful car in the world.

The perfect profile, yet not styled at all; the original wheelbase E-Type in red seen hustling along on wire wheels and in fine fettle. Note the shallow angle to rear roof and deck.

The details of exquisite design: early Series 1 headlamps, sidelamps and taillamps were like items of engineering jewellery in Sayer's hands. Nothing was out of place and every aspect of the design worked.

know, came D-Type, long-nose D-Type, the XKSS derivative of D-Type and then E-Type itself.

Crucially, Sayer took with him to Coventry advanced knowledge of aerodynamics and a little-known tutelage. He had worked at the Bristol Company at the beginning of the Second World War alongside Beverley Shenstone – newly appointed to work closely with Bristol and its directors on wartime engineering projects. Shenstone had been the aerodynamicist on the Supermarine Spitfire and created its shape and the unique (and not Heinkel-derived) double-axis, asymmetric, modified elliptical wing shape that gave the Spitfire its turning and flying advantage over all other fighters. Special curved panels were also created for the Spitfire's wing-to-fuselage conjunction as an aerodynamic fillet device; airflow off the body and tail were also this airframe's specific mastery. The same theories would soon apply to a Jaguar.

The designer of these features, Shenstone, had trained in Germany from 1929 to 1931 with Junkers and with the inventor of the swept delta wing, Lippisch. Shenstone was a top expert and new proponent of elliptical forms and a mathematical design development process. Latterly a contributor to Vickers aviation engineering and a President of the Royal Aeronautical Society and a senior airline figure, he was in 1939 professionally close to Bristol's Sir Roy Fedden and worked on several projects with him, such as the all-wing concept and German aerodynamics technology, through to the Fedden Mission of 1944.

Sayer worked with Shenstone on the same projects at Bristol and heard much of Shenstone's ideas and mathematical approach. Given that the later Jaguar D-Type was shaped from and of the ellipse and even had elliptical structural elements in a semi-monocoque sub-chassis construction, built in alloys (like the Supermarine Spitfire and the Vickers Viscount airliner both had), we can chart a direct elliptical design research process from the Spitfire and Shenstone, through Sayer to the D-Type and thence to the E-Type.

An evidence trail from Supermarine to Bristol to Jaguar is therefore clear amid the E-Type's genes and design process. Ultimately, it would all gel in Jaguar's D-Type, and then via E-Type to the amazing XJ13 which also looked, handled and sounded like a Supermarine Spitfire on wheels.

Like Beverley Shenstone, Malcolm Sayer was a British design and engineering hero who is owed greater recognition. A website has been set up by Sayer's family (championed by his grandson) to celebrate the great man's works, at malcolmsayer.com.

Latterly, in 1966 a shortened E-Type 2+2 prototype was proposed by Sayer in a bid to make a version of the car that was less overtly a supercar sportster: we might opine that it was a good thing it did not go ahead. Interestingly, the Jaguar prototype department had built a special studio bodyshell that could be widened, shortened or lengthened to meet any specific design study ideas.

The original winged wheelnut design on wire wheels, a mechanism soon to be outlawed in 1960s United States and Europe.

Engine and Drivetrain

XK Twin-cam
Originally, Jaguar launched a double overhead camshaft in-line six-cylinder engine in 1949 as British post-war austerity and ration books still ruled, but also at a time when motor sport was re-emerging. It became a 1950s race winner and the basis of the engine used in the E-Type prior to the fitment of the V12 unit.

The in-line six cylinder was the work of several people. Its characteristics include a good torque curve, excellent 'breathing', a refined crank, and a revvy nature that was nevertheless smooth and tractable. A wide-angle cylinder head was fitted to the XK engines seen in the racing D-Types, as were sandcast Weber carburettors. E-Type would benefit from such learning and developments, but the one area where the XK had a limitation was latterly deemed to be the cylinder head angle and its consequences. Twin carbs, triple carbs and in V12 even more carbs? Mechanical

fuel injection? At some stage the various E-Types have tried it all.

Using the XK engine in the launch version of the E-Type was an obvious move. Developing a higher-capacity, better breathing version would come later. If only Lyons had not fitted a mild steel exhaust system that rotted in a few short winters; but there was money in replacement parts.

Jaguar E-Type: Fast Facts
Body: Low drag semi-monocoque with frame-on engine bay system. As two-door open roadster or coupé with glazed rear, hatch opening door feature.
Engine: Straight-six.
S1 with 3,871cc, 256bhp at 5,500rpm (S2 with 4,235cc, 265bhp at 5,400rpm).
Top speed: 149/150mph, 0–60mph in 7 seconds.
Transmission: Manual 4-speed.
Suspension: Independent suspension all round.
Brakes: Discs.
Note: S3 with V12 engine, 5,343cc, 272bhp at 5,850rpm. Top speed 146mph, 0–60mph in 9 seconds. Longer wheelbase.

V12
In 1954, as Britain was producing world-class military and civil aircraft, locomotives and ships, Jaguar, by now famous at Le

This late-1962 car shows how good dark blue can look on an E-Type. Note the chrome windscreen surround which reminds us of the preceding XKSS windscreen frame design by the same designer's hand. Note the early door mirror design and fitting.

Mans, came up with a Ferrari-competing V12 engine of 5.0-litre capacity. Yet it took years for the engine to find a car prototype in which to perform: the amazing XJ13, which was one of Jaguar's greatest lost opportunities and which did not achieve volume status nor mass production. From 1964 through to 1967 and its use in the XJ13, Jaguar's V12 took a long time to reach full production reality.

For the E-Type application the double overhead cam per bank V12 was built not with the double overhead camshaft configuration, but with chain-driven direct single overhead-camshaft per cylinder bank. Initially complicated and heavy, not to mention given to some noisy emanations from deep within its block, the camshaft design modifications with single chain-driven single-cam, new valves and valves springs, created the much-smoother production V12 for the E-Type. The compression ratio was also softened. The effect of these changes amid an increase to 5.3 litres was to soften the engine from a competition type to wider application.

Just shy of a magical 300bhp at 272bhp (with tuned 296bhp known) the other key ingredient from bore, stroke, crank design, valve mechanism, swept volume and the refinements of its mechanical actuation, was that the torque figure matched (or just exceeded) the rated horsepower figure – a true sign of a successful engine design. Smooth, sweet-running, large yet responsive, and above all blessed with minimal mechanical noise, vibration and harshness (NVH), this new V12 engine with its 1950s design origination found its first mass-production Jaguar use in the 1971 E-Type V12. It would of course be fitted into the XJ series cars too, then into the XJ-S as E-Type's replacement, and beyond. Latterly, the improved high efficiency cylinder head with improved combustion swirl-process (via May's design work) aided the V12's rather poor fuel economy.

There is no doubt that despite a very long gestation period, Jaguar had created one of the finest V12 engines ever produced. The 1970s' fuel crisis, BL's woes, strikes and lack of money did not help, but in the end the V12 became a hallmark of Jaguar's excellence. By the end of S3 V12 production in 1975, 14,983 V12 E-Types had been built.

Suspension and Dynamics

Gone was the old 'live' rear axle; in came independent set-up and at the front a double wishbone suspension featured torsion-bar-sprung actuation which fed

The classic stance and scale, with the roadster E-Type seen hood-up.

From the rear, the erect hood had poor aerodynamics but served its purpose. Note the upswept underbody aerodynamic design. E-Type exhausts were subject to design changes in the mid-1960s.

their loadings back into the monocoque tub on the bulkhead. At the rear a coil spring, beam axle set-up amid an independent suspension with subframe mounting upon which the Salisbury-type differential was mounted, also added to axle location amid a bottom wishbone and at the driveshaft as a locating link. Rubber bushes isolated the set-up.

The suspension rack was rubber-bush-mounted which improved shock and vibration absorption but reduced stiffness and steering accuracy. Early E-Types were of course shod with old technology cross-ply Dunlop tyres which were far less compliant than later radial tyres. So, Jaguar's engineers needed to take loads and shock out of the front end and the steering rack by fitting rubber absorbers in the rack. Owners soon grasped that Pirelli's ground-breaking Cinturato-type tyre was a superb upgrade for the E-Type, even if they did soon wear off the tyre shoulders on a hard-cornered E-Type. Keeping the tracking correct was to prove vital.

One of the benefits of the steering set-up was that it offered the driver feel and feedback through the steering column and

steering wheel to inform the driver what was going on with the front wheels and the tyres' interaction with the tarmac. But the rubber mounts were probably more effective in compression on twisting roads rather than tension when the front-end of the car 'lifted' at high speed on a straight road.

The same car's wonderful original interior with red leather and the earlier metal-effect console trim and toggle switches.

This 1966 car is interesting for its wheel type, and the fitted steel 'bubble' hardtop. The symbolic E-Type long bonnet is captured here too.

Hardtop detail. Note the rear window shape and the rarely seen chrome trim at the trailing edge of the side window.

An underbody view shows off the suspension, chassis and floorpan details. Note the floorpan heel wells. (Photo Jaguar)

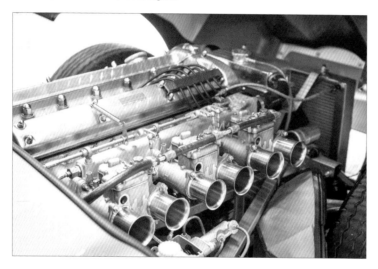

Above: The XK engine as straight-six magic. Note the steel beams of the spaceframe crucible.

Below: Bonnet louvres were vital to remove hot air. Very early cars had them welded into the bonnet panel, but this was soon abandoned in favour of the cheaper and easier-to-make steel pressing with louvres in situ.

different roof and door panels. Change to Jaguar gearbox and full brake servo actuation.

1967
Series 1½ with non-faired headlamps. New US emissions regulations for engine settings.

1968
Series 2 with wraparound bumper, sidelights-below-bumper design. Changes to carburettors. First change to windscreen rake and size via re-roofed 2+2 only.

American safety regulations meant that US-bound E-Types were festooned with extra side indicators, different lamps and trim changes, none of which really ruined

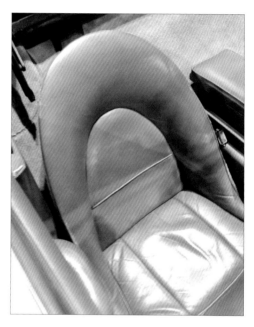

Early E-Type driver's seat design, which was soon changed for something less minimalist.

E-Type Design Timeline

1961
E-Type S1 3.8 litre launched as flat-floor design: built until June 1962 when new stepped floorpan with wheel wells was fitted. Moss-type gearbox and bellows brake vacuum pressure device and external bonnet catches were original specification.

1963
Special 175mph Lightweight cars, twelve cars built.

1964
Series 1 with 4.2-litre engine. Launch of 2+2 long wheelbase fastback only with

The classic command post with wood-rimmed, alloy-spoked wheel with Jaguar legend on the boss.

the car's purity of line, but those front and rear side indicator lenses were unfortunate in their necessary application. Girling brakes replaced Dunlop.

1971

V12 5.3-litre engine cars with longer wheelbase, longer doors, and trim, bumper, lighting and styling modifications plus interior changes.

Right: Modern variation on an original E-Type cabin with recent radio and gearshift. Eagle-eyed readers will know why.

Below: The pure, 1961 original E-Type factory interior with early seats and in left-hand drive too. A defining reference photo for modellers. (Photo Jaguar)

Triple carb delight. Note the Pirelli tyres. This is a Jaguar Classic car. (Photo Jaguar)

More straight-six delight amid exquisite detailing. (Photo Jaguar)

Design detail, the Lightweight-type fittings with drilled steel wheels, and leather bonnet straps shown. (Photo Jaguar)

A March 1969 Series 2 convertible with the revised front lighting treatment and larger intake. Still an essential E-Type even if faired-in headlamps are absent. More power, new gearbox type, better brakes, nicer seats, and easier to drive. This yellow paint was quite a popular hue for the E-Type at the time. Note the curvature of Sayer's side panel design – mathematically calculated.

Different character, the Series 3 coupé on steel wheels, with V12 under the bonnet and a Webasto folding-sunroof above. A different E-Type from 1961, but a great one nonetheless.

Development

Norman Dewis on a development drive on early E-Type at MIRA. Note the black headlamp trims as opposed to chrome. (Photo Jaguar)

Model by Model

Crucial to E-Type was its development process. The car was launched as a flat-floor car in Series 1 form, then a revised floor design was fitted and then a Series 1½ definition specification arrived, then the S2, thence the longer wheelbase S3. Along the way there were variations of specification and differing iterations of engineering (notably the gearbox and brakes) and the body shape, not least the lightweight, low-drag, and the tapered-tail one-off. Engines went from 3.8-litre straight-six, to 4.2-litre (with redesigned block), then to the mighty V12 of 5.3 litres. The 4.2-litre with revised block, head, and camshaft hit 153mph on a test run in 1965.

Certain economy measures in the E-Type's specification and trim saw the early cars use cheap-looking fascia and console alloy trim, latterly replaced with wood veneer.

The steering rack was 'soft' as it had basic rubber mounts that reduced accuracy. Improving these rubber mounts and the steering rack are often a latter-day E-Type improvement. The bought-in Moss gearbox was to be replaced by a Jaguar all-synchromesh item and the early brake bellows vacuum pedal assister replaced.

For all his excellence, Sir William sometimes curtailed costs and quality at the expense of performance car standards, yet soon upgraded any recalcitrant items. Rust-proofing was notable by its absence: Sir William achieved production costs savings in certain areas.

An interesting development in 1968 was the enlarging of the signature front air vent/radiator inlet grille area design. This let over 60 percent more airflow into the engine bay and reduced the E-Type's heat soak issue. It may have also benefitted the aerodynamics too by reducing lift.

Many improvements and specification changes were made and production cycle changes were manifested across the E-Type series. Of note, the higher roof line and reframed windscreen of the 2+2 coupé detracted from the original coupé's roof and fastback styling and affected its aerodynamics, but it still sold well.

Genesis: 1957–1958

The first E-Type began prototype build in late 1957. Significantly, the very first E-Type design prototype was E1A of early 1958 final build and was a 2.4-litre alloy-bodied car. E2A was a 3.8-litre car of alloy body type and a competition prototype. Chassis #850001 was a pre-production prototype with a roadster body and chassis #850002 was fitted with more than one experimental gearbox type. The famous E-Type 77RW was the first true production demonstrator car as chassis #850003 and #850004 was 1600RW – latterly owned by F.R.W. England.

The open or roadster version of the E-Type was launched two weeks after the coupé or fixed-head model. New York's Auto Show was the venue and America took the open car to its heart.

By 1964 the 4.2-litre version of Series 1 was launched with several design changes.

Built from October 1964 to December 1967, these larger-engined S1 cars formed an interesting step up for the model. In 1968 Jaguar readied the 4.2-litre Series 2 with exposed non-faired headlamps, bigger bumpers, and cabin safety changes and much-improved drivetrain engineering. Prior to the introduction of the longer and more powerful Series 3 in 1971, 57,220 of the early series E-Types had been manufactured – an astounding figure for Jaguar.

The 1971 Series 3 cars were the original V12 Jaguars – not the 1972-launched V12-engined XJ saloon as some suggest. The XJ's V12 engine was revised in 1973 and taken to 299bhp in the 'HE' version of 1981, then becoming the true V12 'Soveriegn' of the late 1980s and as V12 up to its demise as late as the 1993 model year. But it was in the 5.3-litre E-Type V12 that a new chapter was born for the model. Of note, the longer wheelbase and cabin floor meant that an automatic gearbox (so vital to US sales) could now be fitted to the open car, not just the longer-wheelbase 2+2 coupé of the previous model line-up.

This, the Series 3 V12 E-Type, was a different type of car yet still continued the Jaguar sporting line that had started with two-door coupés back in late 1934: a larger front air intake orifice, too much added chrome trim (including door fillets), pressed steels and disc-type wheels (wire wheels were available). The US market cars were sadly to be festooned with large (and heavy) bumper over-riders in order to meet the strict new low-speed impact regulations. Different seat trims, new headrests, the rear seats, all created a fundamental shift of E-Type ethos towards a sporting grand tourer or true GT niche in the marketplace. Yet the car could still nudge 145 mph, a sub-9 second 0–60mph sprint, and

Above: A red E-Type roadster cornering hard. Capturing the essence of the E-Type and all it meant in a great British era of car design. (Photo Jaguar)

Right: An elegant early E-Type SI coupé squats as it snarls away from a Bicester Heritage Centre Scramble Day. A red E-Type was the dream of many a schoolboy and remains an enthusiast's apogee.

The open car in opalescent metallic light blue remains an E-Type favourite. With hood folded away and trimmed in dark blue, this was the 1960s icon at its most famous.

Jaguar Classic recently built E-Type continuations, an electrically powered version ... silver-blue dream machines perhaps ought to be of combustive powerplant however.

possessed the incredible smoothness of the V12 engine and its drivetrain delivery. Fuel consumption of 12–17mpg in focused driving was however to be an issue and getting to over 20 mpg in touring driving required a lighter right foot.

The global fuel crisis of 1973/74 effectively killed off the coupé's sales basis yet the roadster remained in production for longer – surviving in showroom sales terms just beyond to the opening of 1975. The final fifty V12 roadsters benefitted from a black finish (forty-nine out of the fifty), special trims (a cast plaque bearing Sir William's signature) and, of interest, a smartly timed hardtop that really did lend a more modern design feel to the car. Just for once the car looked very good with its hardtop fitted. The last E-Type built was registered as HDU 555N and retained by the factory.

One significance, almost 85 percent of E-Type production was actually exported and today, many left-hand drive (LHD) cars have been converted to right-hand drive (RHD) – increasing the numbers of RHD cars in comparison to factory records.

Of little-known fact was that in the late 1960s, Jaguar looked at a heavily revised version of the E-Type that would be easier to use by being shorter and more economical. Sayer and Lyons created a shorter E-Type that used the long doors and cabin of the 2+2 mated to a truncated nose section housing a smaller engine. It was a concept that did not come to fruition. Often overlooked are the standard production cars lightly modified by John Coombs (1922–2013) at his dealership for private customers. From fast-engine engine modifications and changes to steering rack to suspension, Coombs tweaked several ingredients: competition Restall-type seats and revised switch gear could also be fitted. Jaguar's Mk 1 and Mk 2 cars often got the Coombs treatment too – with added spats and vents to cool the harder-working engine (Lotus leader Colin Chapman ran one such Mk 2). And Coombs lent his Ferrari 250 GTO to Browns Lane so that Jaguar could check out its main racing competitor

Hurtling along, hood up. Note flat-front non-faired headlamps and black-painted wire wheels as differences.

The classic cockpit: a recent Jaguar Classic E-Type interior with trim differences to the centre console but lots of dials and switches – pure 1960s cabin comfort.

It is recorded that some of Coombs' earliest E-Type modifications were applied to dark blue E-Type registration 9 VPD as chassis #850007 as part of the ZPS/37 project (see below).

In later years, Coombs owned his own personally modified E-Type with flared arches, D-Type camshaft profiles and many engine details improved and, of note, a Broad Speed-type gearbox.

By 1964, trying to keep the E-Type up with the Ferraris, Coombs further modified his team cars with high-lift camshafts, new wheels and differing suspension rates. A certain young driver named Jackie Stewart, who had a very smooth driving style, soon powered the E-Type to new top speeds on the circuit, notably at Brands Hatch.

A close-up of an in-use 1962 car shows the metal-effect console trim and early cabin specifications. The vital rpm dial is red-lined from 5,500 rpm.

Motor-sport E-Type: Low Weight, Low Drag and the ZP 537 Cars

Two vital chapters in the E-Type' legend were the Low Drag coupé and the Lightweight cars. Descriptions between the two can become confused as the Lightweights also had aerodynamic drag-reduction body modifications, and two of the Lightweights were converted to differing variations of the original, single Low Drag E-Type.

Prior to Jaguar investing in further E-Type development, privateer customers such as Jaguar dealer John Coombs had with chassis 850006 with Roy Salavdori driving, up against Graham Hill in Jaguar dealer Tommy Sopwith's E-Type #850005 at Oulton Park. Such early outings suggested track-focused E-Type developments. Coombs converted E-Type #850006 to lightweight specification as #850658.

Sopwith had received one of the first E-Types to be delivered, registered ECD 400 with Hill driving but Coombs soon offered Hill a drive. It is to Coombs that we look to see that without his ideas and drive, the motor-sport E-Type derivatives might never have developed as they did, or even

at all. Some say he, or his effect, inspired and pushed Jaguar into making such E-Types. Coombs had had his own motor-sport career on the circuit prior to running his own team and Jaguar modification outfit which included purchasing five spare D-Types direct from Jaguar. It was Coombs who pressured Jaguar into making a lighter, faster E-Type to attack the Ferraris with – of that most writers agree.

ZP537/24

Jaguar engineer Derrick White had suggested a run of lighter sports-special E-Types for competition purposes. Lyons quietly agreed to seven special E-Types being built as special project cars under the factory nomenclature of ZP537/24. These cars had tuned engines with lightened and coated internal components. Gas-flowed-heads, lightened flywheel, special crankshaft fittings and a close-ratio gearbox all added to their speed. Revised, stiffer suspension reduced roll.

Use of Dunlop racing tyres of differing aspect ratio and construction somewhat reduced the early cross-ply-type tyre issues. Jaguar released these race-spec cars onto the competition arena as the E-Type was launched, as teasers for the E-Type. Significantly, Graham Hill was an E-Type ZP driver and won an event at Oulton Park circuit in early 1961, one month after the E-Type's official launch at the Geneva Motor Show. In the ZP project cars began the thinking for a developed racing E-Type. Next up came the single Low Drag coupé and then the twelve Lightweight roadsters.

Low Drag Coupé

This was an attempt to create a high-speed racer out of the baseline of E-Type ingredients. As quickly as twenty-four months into production, an E-Type with major revisions to its bodywork appeared. This included a costly new windscreen, frame, A-pillars, roof and turret/tail structure. Thinner metal was used for

Chassis #850003 or 77RW, the first demo car seen restored and with a well-known and expert Jaguar commentator aboard. Chassis #850004 was registered as 1600RW. (Photo Jaguar)

the body panels to save weight. Shaped by Malcolm Sayer and not intended for volume production, this was the first one-off E-Type Special which Sayer christened the 'Low drag car'.

Sayer reckoned that he could add a few miles an hour to the terminal velocity and reduce lift without creating extra drag or an airflow bow wave over the car from added spoilers. The ideas of John Coombs for a racing E-Type were not unrelated either via the Lightweight E-Types as he was a key figure in non-factory development of enhanced states of tune and specifications for Jaguar Mk1/Mk2 and E-Type.

Aluminium panels were added to the base E-Type and a new windscreen of greater curvature leading into a domed roof and shallow angle tail greatly improved airflow over the car's turret. The windscreen seemed to match aerodynamic shapes also to be seen at Bristol, Panhard and at Citroën – where aerodynamics research would produce similar solutions.

The most notable difference in the design was the tail end – with an attractive rear windscreen shape flowing down to a slightly V-shaped tail inside the raised rear-wing panel lines – each rear-wing line acting as an airflow guide and vortex controller. Although there was no Kamm-type ridge to separate the airflow, Sayer had designed in his airflow and wake vortex points. An inset, transom-like boxed rear valance with number plate recess had a hidden, secret aerodynamic function to tune the airflow off the rear valance. The rear lamp clusters were seen to act as beneficial airflow triggers but adding a small ridge on the rump may have been a step too far.

The engine saw more use of aluminium in its construction (alloy block) as used on the E-Type E2A prototype for competitive outings in 1960. The engine's internals were blueprinted, finished and detailed.

Norman Dewis did much of the E-Type's development driving and tuft-testing with Sayer observing from another vehicle and with photographs being taken. Small changes were thus made to improve the airflow and reduce lift and turbulence in localized areas. Dewis recalled (to the author) that: 'Sticking tufts on the bodywork and observing their flow behaviour was a cheap, cheerful and remarkablly effective means of testing.'

E-Type in different mood: the silver-grey coupé displays the ultimate design sculpture of its era. (Photo Jaguar)

The same car with faired-in headlamps at the front and a 4.2 badge at the back. Note the upswept rear underbody and exhaust work. The oft-ignored rear hatch-type door and elegant window on the fastback section are obvious. (Photo Jaguar)

Above: Low Drag delight. But get those mushroom-headed rivets! Smoothing them off may have been too much. The sleek Sayer lines of the fastback show off the major aerodynamic changes to this car. (Photo Jaguar)

Right: 924 FXC: this car with its longer prow and narrower intake is unusual in that it is a developed Low Drag version and not to be confused with 49 FXN which was an aerodynamically revised non-works conversion of a Lightweight E-Type.

The aerodynamics-related increase in top speed over a standard E-Type coupé was reckoned to be about 10mph which was good but perhaps not as much as Sayer might have hoped for, but it did prove his theories and was a 'free' gain. Here was the true 155–160mph E-Type. Anecdotal reports of it approaching 170mph also exist.

In comparison to the subsequent Lightweight bubbletop E-Type cars, the fuel filler was kept flush on the boot deck to avoid triggering local airflow into turbulence.

Only one original Low Drag coupé was built and registered as CUT 7 after sale by Jaguar to a privateer racer – R. Protheroe – in 1963.

Subsequently, two of the Lightweight bubbletop hardtop E-Types were converted to Low Drag coupé body specification.

Low Weight Type as Lightweight E-Type
The low-weight or Lightweight hardtop (bubbletop) E-Type was based on the open roadster body design but with the addition of the standard metal hardtop of 'bubble' profile and lighter, alloy body skinning. The car was just over 100 kg lighter than a standard-production E-Type – the weight of a large person.

There were, however, some noticeable aerodynamic addenda to be fitted – real stick-on parts that Sayer might not have had. In later 1962 John Coombs was to be the driving force behind private development of such a tuned and modified E-Type, with a weight-reduction programme using alloy parts in place of many steel Jaguar pressings. An alloy blueprinted engine specification and 296bhp were significant performance factors. A five-speed box was also created. But was 350bhp achieved for the race engine? Many think it was.

The Lightweight E-type was powered by a highly developed version of Jaguar's straight-six XK engine which, with its chain-driven twin overhead camshafts and aluminium head with hemispherical combustion chambers, remained advanced in 1964 even though it had first been conceived in 1947. This was the engine that had powered the C- and D-Types to five Le Mans victories in the 1950s; the unit was developed for the Lightweight E-Type based on the 3,868cc engine which in the D-Type had won Le Mans in 1957. A larger-valved, wider-angled cylinder head was fitted in comparison to the standard E-Type head, but in place of the D-type's cast-iron block, Jaguar introduced an aluminium block for the Lightweight E-type which crucially reduced the amount of weight over the front wheels and altered the car's centre of gravity. Another major feature transferred from the D-Type to the Lightweight was the dry sump lubrication system with revised oil pumps to reduce surging during cornering. (A semi-lightweight E-Type was also created during this process.)

The likes of Graham Hill, Stirling Moss and Roy Salvadori were to make competitive marks with these lightweight cars in 1963. Brian Redman would in 1965 drive the Coombs car. It was probably regrettable yet fortuitous fate that by this time Sydney Allard had ceased racing and car production, for he would have shown the E-Type a thing or two on the track, especially if he had built more than just the one Jaguar XK-powered Allard GT coupé, and if his plan to use that engine in late-1950s production had come to fruition.

The German Jaguar distributor Peter Lindner was fundamental in campaigning the Lightweight E-Type, so too was the American Briggs Cunningham who ran more than one E-Type Lightweight roadster in his private team of white cars with twin blue-striped livery. Cunningham drove the E-Type EA prototype at Le Mans as early as 1960; Cunningham then ran three production E-type chassis – #850659, #850664 and #850665 – all as Lightweight specification types. His cars raced at Sebring and at Le Mans in 1963. Cunningham's first E-Types Lightweight runs were conducted by Ed Leslie and Frank Morrill at Sebring who took the car to a Class win and seventh overall.

French racer Pierre Bardinon decided that the E-Type coupé's better aerodynamics were key to racing speed and he converted such a car to near or semi-Lightweight specification in 1964.

Two Fastback Specials

We should recall that two of the Lightweight types were converted to a very similar specification to the one-off fastback original Sayer Low Drag coupé. Of particularly note was one of these examples that benefitted from aerodynamics research and engine and chassis developments carried out not by Jaguar, but by a private group. This single prototype was based on the race-crashed remains of a car raced by Messrs Lumsden and Sargent. A Dr S. Klat of Imperial College London is credited with aspects of the design's aero development.

This car featured an even more curved windscreen than the Low Drag coupé

The open car was the basis of the Lightweight which was fitted with the metal hardtop and numerous vents, aerodynamic fences, alloy panels and leather straps. (Photo Jaguar)

From the rear, bodywork changes and addenda are obvious. Note the body seams and roof and boot vents and ridges. The Lightweights were over 100kg lighter and of course featured significant engine and drivetrain modifications. (Photo Jaguar)

Sir Stirling Moss and Win Percy drove this Lightweight EOL 584C to great effect – recently campaigned across the historic scene. This E-Type is in fact a later, 1990 conversion of a 1965 S1 Semi-Lightweight specification car. The famed RS Panels company oversaw the 're-originalisation'.

EOL 584C Lightweight in detail: ultra-smooth fairings reduced drag triggers on the car's nose.

and another different roof profile. The car's nose cone was lengthened and the intake size reduced. With attention to reducing lift off the rear roof and tail, and to tuning vortices under the car, early advances in ground effect were explored. How much the prior aerodynamic Lister-Jaguar and Frank Costin's aero design work contributed is worth noting. Major improvements also took place to the internal specifications of the engine components including mechanical fuel injection – alongside the aero package.

For Jaguar and its new E-Type, further motor-sport focus came early in the E-Type's lifecycle after the prototype car chassis # E2A (registered as VKV752) was raced by Cunningham at Le Mans in 1960. As we know, the production E-Type won its first event at Oulton Park in 1961 conducted by a certain Graham Hill, then came the John Coombs E-Type (of factory rather than dealership modification) which was also at some stage driven by Hill. This inspired the ZP537/24 cars and the twelve Lightweight cars.

By 1964, Hill had won on multiple occasions driving one form of E-Type or another. Roy Salavdori drove the E-Type roadster registered BUY1 in 1961 (also to be registered as 4WPD) in national class events. Kjell Qvale also drove a Lightweight in American competition. Famous British Grand Prix driver Innes Ireland raced an E-Type and we should not forget that Peter Sargent was fifth at Le Mans in a Lightweight (with P. Lumsden) latterly to be converted to a coupé body car.

Of interest, Jaguar (Browns Lane) employee and development engineer Peter Taylor raced his own E-Type and won the British production-car championship in his cleverly tweaked E-Type 2+2 coupé. In fact, Taylor's car was a works' prototype 2+2 for the Series 3 yet which had been engineered to take the XK engine but later sold as a V12 to Taylor. Of note, a very few XK 4.2-litre Series 3 cars were manufactured.

In 1963 Robert Jane won the 1963 Australian GT Championship in an E-Type Lightweight. In 1965 Murray Rainey, the three-times Australian Formula 3 champion of the 1950s, imported an E-Type for racing in Australia and in 1974 his daughter Joy Rainey won many national club-level events, notably in the hill-climb class in her red E-Type coupé. Today, E-Types still compete in hill-climb classes at locations such as Prescott.

Across the 1960s, privateers, garagistes and well-heeled Americans and Europeans raced E-Types, but we might argue that the racing V12 Series 3 E-Types campaigned in America during 1974–6 by Robert Tullius and Lee Mueller gave a late renaissance to the legend of the E-Type as a competitive car even if it was under British Leyland's overarching banner and effect.

Names such as Bruce McLaren and Mike Parkes won with the E-Type at major British events; the E-Type went to Spa-Francorchamps in Belgium but only came second due to a lack of ultimate top speed against the Ferraris. The XK engine was better suited to A- and B-road lunging through the gears as bends were parried though, rather than flat-out terminal-velocity runs on a racing straight.

More recently, classic and historic racing classes have seen E-Types of all incarnations compete at Goodwood, Silverstone, Snetterton and at overseas circuits as far afield as America and Australia as well as in Europe.

The details were stunning. The fuel filler cap is one for the modellers to study.

The Lightweight had special wheels and a winged hub nut with three, not two, fittings.

The windscreen pillar chrome fillets were not just trims, they were a small aero gain on the difficult-to-achieve windscreen-to-side-panel transition.

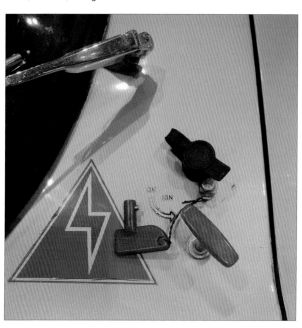

Emergency switches to cut off power in case of an event … super detailing for modellers.

Left: Drilled panels added lightness to alloyed parts. Venting helped internal flow and ridges on the roof and boot lid benefitted external airflow separation.

Below: The motor-sport branding font of JAGUAR. Enough said, surely …

The interior had several trim differences and a roll-bar and fire-suppression system. This command post meant business.

A coupé as semi-Lightweight specification in silver-blue – the best of both worlds? (Photo Jaguar)

E-Type: Details of Development

Jaguar E-Type: detailed model history/variants

1961–1964

E-Type Series 1, 3.8-litre Open Two-seater Convertible and Coupé Types

Built from March 1961 to October 1964 with both body types from launch.

3,781cc straight-six engine.

Max speed: 150mph (145mph cited by enthusiasts in normal used spec).

Built with early bonnet side-lock type until October 1961.

Note: flat-floor E-Type roadster and fixed-head coupé built without foot-wells (for lower legs/heels), until June 1962 to chassis numbers #850358/#876582 (open) and #860176/#885504 (coupé). Thence built with dropped floor for lower foot room and better driving position. Fitted with Moss-type gearbox, and a bellows brake vacuum pressure device. Dynamo electric supply on very early cars.

Note: Early batch of cars with welded-in bonnet louvres: later cars with pressed bonnet moulding. External bonnet locks modified.

Early cars with Dunlop cross-ply tyres. Radials latterly fitted.

Long tail-type exhaust silencers fitted until October 1963. Three windscreen wipers fitted after first production chassis. Badging and trim specification changes during 1963–4.

Open convertible: 942 RHD, 6,885 LHD built.

Fixed-head coupé: 1,798 RHD, 5,971 LHD built.

1963–1964

E-Type 'Lightweight' Series 1, Two-seater (Hardtop)

Built from March 1963 to January 1964.

3,781cc straight-six engine, revised cylinder head, fuel injection, dry sump type, four-speed or optional five-speed gearbox.

Max speed: 175mph.

Built with aluminium body panel construction and fixed (alloy) hardtop with venting to rear top section and to boot lid. Bonnet with fixed side catches. Dunlop centre-peg-type wheels and mounting. Bumpers deleted.

Chassis number #S850006 and thence from #S860659.

All RHD, 12 built. (Note: subsequent continuation chassis built).

1964–1967

E-Type Series 1, 4.2-litre Open Two-seater Roadster and Coupé Types, with 2+2 Long-wheelbase Coupé

Built from October 1964 to December 1967.

4,235cc engine.

Max speed: 140mph.

Identical to Series 1 3.8-litre. Chassis numbers from #1E1001/#1E75001. Jaguar all-synchromesh gearbox fitted. Vacuum brake bellow deleted, new brake actuation. Minor cabin trim changes (black trim replaced anodized). Revised seat design and alterations to wire wheel/hub design in May 1967. Badging/nomenclature changes to read E-Type 4.2.

Open car chassis numbers from #1E1001/#1E75001.

Coupé chassis numbers from #1E20001/#1E30001.

Open convertible: 883 RHD, 5,579 LHD built.

Fixed-head coupé: 1,583 RHD built, 5,582 LHD built.

Variant: 2+2 Long-wheelbase Coupé

Built from March 1966 to September 1968 as first E-Type bodyshell variation development.

Lower max speed: 135mph.

Coupé with new higher roof line, change to windscreen and rake, 9-inch wheelbase extension with longer doors and two rear seats for 2+2 four-seat accommodation. Chrome in-fill to door top. Glovebox lockers fitted. Minor trim changes. Automatic transmission option.

2+2 coupé chassis numbers #1E50001/#1E75001.

974 RHD built, 2,708 LHD built.

Note: Prior to introduction of the Series 1½, a low number of open-headlamp-type Series 1 cars were built with unique fittings and some Series overlap is suggested in late 1967.

1967–1968

E-Type Series 1½, 4.2-litre Open Two-seater Convertible and Coupé Types, with 2+2 Long-wheelbase Coupé

Series 2 coupé, in motor-sport competition trim and seen at Prescott Hill Climb. Note the larger front intake.

Left: S2 roadster in primrose-yellow legend: a different side to E-Type's character, but a valuable one.

Below: Despite styling changes to the headlamps, front and rear sidelamps, rear brake lights and larger bumpers, the revised E-Type retained its allure. The haunched rear end and elliptically shaped trailing edge to the body remained design hallmarks.

Built from September 1967 to October 1968.

4,235cc engine, with change from triple to twin carburettors.

Interim model development prior to official Series 2: manufactured with un-faired, upright open-lens headlamps set onto wing line with chrome trims. General trim changes include new fascia, rocker switches replacing toggles, revised materials and badges. Reclining seats. Revised door panels. Special road wheel external hubs on US and German export models due to regulation changes. Winged spinner deleted for new hub nut type.

2+2 continues with Series 1 2+2-type windscreen and A-pillar design and with automatic transmission option which reduces top speed to 130mph.

Open car chassis numbers from #1E1864/ #1E15980.

Coupé chassis numbers from #1E21584/ #1E34583.

2+2 coupé chassis numbers from #1E50975/ #1E77709.

Open convertible: 319 RHD, 2,387 LHD built.

Fixed-head coupé: 374 RHD, 271 LHD built.

Fixed-head 2+2 coupé: 404 RHD built, 1,512 LHD built.

1968–1970

E-Type Series 2, 4.2-Litre Open Two-seater Convertible and Coupé Types, with 2+2 Long-Wheelbase coupé

Built from October 1968 to September 1970.

4,235cc engine.

Revised model with full-width bumpers and larger oval front air intake aperture. New front and rear indicator and stop lamp design and locations. Twin-electric cooling fans fitted. Open headlamps with revised mounting (forwards). New alternator type fitted. Earless spinners to wire wheels from March 1969. Revised (splayed) exhaust tailpipes. Revised badging and Jaguar logos. Larger sidelights/re-positioned. Brake servo mechanism improved.

Open car chassis numbers from #1R1001/ #1R7001.

Coupé chassis numbers from #1R20001/ #1R25001.

2+2 chassis numbers from #1R35001/ #1R40001.

Open convertible: 785 RHD, 7,852 LHD built.

Fixed-head coupé: 1,070 RHD, 3,785 LHD built.

Fixed-head 2+2 coupé: 1,040 RHD, 4,286 LHD built.

Note: 2+2 features revised windscreen shape and angle – with windscreen to front of scuttle line. 9-inch extension to wheelbase and revised roof profile as per earlier Series 2+2.

Design differences. The coupé seen beside the roadster (hood up). Readers can reach their own decision as to preference … the coupé was much better aerodynamically.

Right: The longer wheelbase arrived in the 2+2 coupé, with a higher roof line and revised glazing.

Below: The classic profile – and winged wheel nuts.

Although not the purist's choice, the S3 deserves its following and for many years provided a cheaper way into E-Type ownership. Later SIII V12 roadsters had a very nice hardtop design.

1971–1975

E-Type Series 3, 5.3-litre V12 Open Two-seater Convertible Long Wheelbase, and 2+2 Long-wheelbase Coupé

Built as an open convertible from March 1971 to late 1974 with final cars to February 1975. Coupé built from March 1971 to September 1973.

5,343-cc V12 engine of single overhead camshaft per bank type. Black ribbed engine cover.

Note: A small number of 4.2-litre engine, early Series 3 cars built.

Convertible and coupé: Final bodyshell with standardized long wheelbase (8ft 9in). Flared front and rear wheel arches to accommodate wider wheel and tyre section of 6x15. Larger front grille oval section with slatted type design. New rear lamps in under-bumper valance, with full-width rear bumper type. Wire wheels latterly to be replaced by pressed-steel type with chrome embellishers. Fishtail-type four-exhaust tailpipes replaced by twin pipes in 1973. Revised windscreen shaper and angle: twin wipers instead of three. Air-conditioning option. Extra side indicators to US specification.

Open car chassis numbers from #1S1001/ #1S2001.

Coupé chassis numbers from #1S50001/ #1S7001.

Open convertible: 1,871 RHD, 6,119 LHD built.

Fixed-head 2+2 coupé: 2,115 RHD, 5,182 LHD built.

Of interest, the majority of E-Type sales were overseas with only 12,330 E-Types originally being UK-spec right-hand drive out of 72,529 cars built. Total Production of all models: 72, 529. (One later S3 roadster was constructed from leftover genuine factory parts as the R. Parrott car.)

In design development terms, was the purist S1 E-Type the early 3.8-litre flat-floor car as so many say, and as values indicate? But what of the rare 4.2-litre S1 model years 1965–1967 when S1 retained its looks but got more power and a better gearbox? Perhaps here lies an E-Type grail?

S1 cars fall into two divisions, being those made between 1961 and 1964, which had 3.8-litre engines and the early (limited) synchromesh transmission, and the S1½ cars which benefitted from the increased engine capacity and the new fully synchronized transmission, yet kept the faired-in headlamp style and S1 trims. Transition cars from S1½ to the full S2 (non-faired headlamps etc.) do, as we know, exist in even smaller numbers than originally made. Therefore, we should note the very few S1 cars from the last weeks of production of the S1, that there were a small number of cars produced that had the faired-in headlight covers removed yet retained all other prior specifications. We should further note that the chrome fillets and fittings for these lamps were different to those fitted to the next series as S2, yet which appeared to be almost identical.

Driving the E-Type: S1 Classicism?

Approach the long low sculpture, peel open the door, slide your legs down and in via swivelling on the seat, settle in between the close-fitting door and the transmission tunnel behind that big upright wheel and you are in the cocoon. Start up, circulate and warm the oil for a couple of minutes. Gently and lightly grip the big alloy-spoked, wood-rimmed steering wheel with that wonderful Jaguar badge on its hub, release the very odd-looking long-handled handbrake and deliberately engage the gear required – but do it slowly.

Then you are off and, once warmed, the engine and gearbox allow rapid progress. The world seems to zoom towards you in cinemascope-type perspective through the curved yet narrow-depth windscreen portal. The dashboard is up close, your legs stretched out ahead. Heat begins to soak through the footwells and transmission tunnel.

Ease the gear changes, watch out for baulking of the shift: place the car accurately with minimal steering corrections, don't saw at the wheel. Be smooth and accelerate once out of bend, not via on-off-on throttle behaviour. Keep the car, the braking and the power linear and stable, but use the XK engine's power to lunge between bends and overtaking manoeuvres. The engine snarls rather than rasps (V12s rumble with a smoother feel). The car is pointy and accurate. You can tell this car is light though. Then there is the reality of that top-speed potential – something unusual in the car's heyday.

E-Type progress is rapid, stunning and if correctly carried out, smooth. Yet the

steering can be a touch vague on early cars. It is best to know that the steering rack and its mountings are correct or, better still, upgraded, for the truth is that the steering on early E-Types is not as accurate as later, more developed series cars. The handling limits are high but not infallible, notably if on old part-worn cross ply, or all three issues of tyres. Pirellis or

Top: The extra height to the coupé 2+2 and S3 coupé body via a longer and taller cabin turret section is clearly seen in this shot – as is the revised front grille design. (Photo Jaguar)

Above: S3 tail amid E-Type line-up shows off the stages of design changes to E-Type. (Photo Jaguar)

The last E-Type built – an S3 V12 roadster with the revised hardtop design. One of fifty, this car was retained by Jaguar. (Photo Jaguar)

The Lister-Jaguar with independent aerodynamics changes. Note the very smooth windscreen glass and roof panel transition details. (Photo Jaguar)

One of the recent Jaguar Classic series as a Lightweight specification car. Note standard-type boot lid but propped open. (Photo Jaguar)

The famous CUT 7 Low Drag fastback as modified (E.R. Protheroe, chassis #860004) follows a Lightweight in classic Jaguar motor-sport action.

racing tyres help location and feedback but do not last long at all. Watch out for a slightly skittish rear end if you push hard, especially in the wet but such limits are not critical in normal driving, for E-Type brought in new standards of handling for Jaguar and for such cars.

In 1961, the steering and the handling were, however, advances for Jaguar and for such type of car, as was the 149–150mph possibility. Brakes? Early cars had less-effective brakes and this is best to bear in mind if emergency retardation is needed. You almost wonder if the system was speed-calibrated: slower speed – slower brakes.

Driving the first Series is a pure E-Type experience; driving the 4.2-litre S2 is actually nicer, more accurate and ultimately faster; driving the S3 V12 is another experience, being less visceral but more comfortable, more bearable, requiring less ultimate driver ability and focus, yet no less of a drive.

But whatever the mark of E-Type, the experience is special, defining, characterful and so very different from an electronic modern car of digital authoritarianism. Here in E-Type, notably in the behaviour and sheer character of the S1 or S2, there lies a unique motoring experience to be found. Seen from today's perceptions, the E-Type, notably in early guise, might seem less than perfect in handling and stopping terms, but in its day it was the benchmark road-going performance drive; it changed the motoring public's perception of car design and sports car driving and it was faster than anything else street legal.

As such, E-Type was and remains a sublime classic. That the likes of the more recent Eagle E-Type have addressed the original E-Type's quality and engineering issues born from its initial parsimony of costing, does not undermine the original's status as a defining work. And was any other car, even an Aston, a Ferrari or a Porsche 911, as cool, as utterly stunning to see, be seen in or to command?

Below: 4WPD in profile at high speed. Note the fixed hardtop roof but without roof ridge vent, boot ridge or front wheel arch modification. The driver is clearly a lightweight young Graham Hill with aerodynamic moustache.

The same car in action with Graham Hill at the wheel. Note the external bonnet catches.

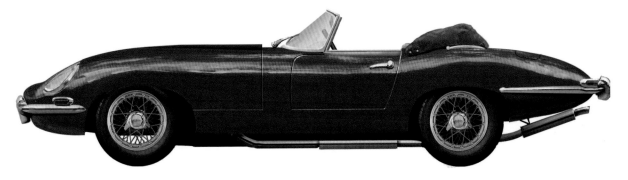

The essential S1 E-Type XK-engined roadster depicted in red, as so many say it should be (unless British Racing Green is desired). In this side profile, we see all the elements of Malcolm Sayer's mathematical design for the bodywork as he calculated and scaled as an industrial design exercise rather than a piece of fashionable styling. The upswept rear bodywork and undertray is evident for its aerodynamic purpose. With XK engine snarling and hood down, a red E-Type was a defining 1960s moment.

The slim, ellipsoid nature of the E-Type design captured from the front. The faired-in headlamps were an expensive yet effective aerodynamic solution that also added design language. From intake to windscreen, every design element worked to create an appropriately feline one-piece.

Seen from overhead, the E-Type was less curvaceous. The lobed corners aided airflow entry and exit patterns and the side panels kept flow smooth. Sayer reputedly wanted a more curved windscreen but costs and then-current technology precluded fitting one.

E-Type badging soon usurped the Jaguar branding on the tail of E-Types. Early cars wore Jaguar badges, later S1- and S1½ proclaimed E-Type Jaguar with the car before the marque. 4.2 badging arrived with the engine-capacity increase. The exhaust pipe fantail was subject to several design changes.

A rarer sight was an E-Type S1 Roadster with the metal hardtop fitted. Offered on E-Type from launch, this top was also the type fitted to the Lightweight and Semi-Lightweight E-Types. It offered marginally better aerodynamics than the hood-down or hood-up iterations. An interesting addition on the hardtop was the chromed 'S-iron'-shaped side fitting which hinted at coachbuilt hood techniques of old. No real roll-over protection was offered by the steel hardtop and an internal roll bar was fitted for competitive use. Fitting and using the hardtop tended to scratch the body paint and owners soon fitted body-coloured protective tape where the roof and main body touched.

Early E-Type Roadster soft top hoods (as depicted here) used a 'Twillfast' material that became elastic with use and had a 'Mohair' type ingredient. Later S1 and S2 cars used the 'Everflex' type vinyl material made by Wardle Ltd which better retained its shape and tension. Later E-Types in the USA including S3, could be fitted with a hood made from 'Haartz' branded material. The original Roadster's hood rear window was non-openable but a later zippered window was an after- market offering. When erect, the hood offered weather proofing to occupants but limited visibility somewhat.

One Low Drag E-Type was created by Sayer and Jaguar in 1962 in coupé form; lighter, sleeker, with major revisions to the front and rear bodywork to reduce drag and lift, the car also had a more domed roof panel. Top speed went up by over 10mph. An aluminium alloy version of the 3.8-litre XK engine was fitted. Sayer's desire for a more curved windscreen was achieved. Jaguar had created a faster, lighter, more slippery E-Type for racing development. Confusingly, two further Low Drag-type coupés were privately created from conversions of E-Type Lightweight roadsters. One, 46 FXN (known as the Lumsden/Sargent car), saw further aero work by Dr S. Klat. This featured bodywork changes, a domed roof and windscreen differences and was even more efficient. Although Jaguar was not involved, its chief designer Sayer was reputedly happy to support the further low-drag experimentation of this car.

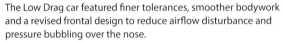

The Low Drag car featured finer tolerances, smoother bodywork and a revised frontal design to reduce airflow disturbance and pressure bubbling over the nose.

A higher rear deck and upswept undertray reduced lift and added downforce. Better control of airflow and vortices off the car gave it an aerodynamic advantage – as did a lighter, more powerful engine.

The Lightweight E-Type was born from Jaguar dealer John Coombs' experimentation and modification ideas; some observers say it was also influenced by internal Jaguar ZP project racing thoughts for E-Type in 1961 – which were then abandoned due to regulatory changes by the racing authorities. Sometimes called the Special GT E-Type, the lightened bodywork and revised engine and suspension stemmed from Coombs' ideas. Coombs had racing experience and had built up a small racing team. His drivers would include Roy Salavdori, an emergent Graham Hill and a young Jackie Stewart. Alloy parts replaced many steel parts and a fixed hardtop added some rigidity. Nearly 50bhp more was secured from the alloy-spec XK engine over the standard production unit. Twelve such cars were built. The white Lightweight with blue stripes depicted here was run by the famous American racer Briggs Cunningham.

Briggs Cunningham ran two then three such Lightweights including at Sebring in 1963 and also at Le Mans where He drove one himself to a top-ten place. A fuel-injected Lightweight coupé in white with blue stripes was also built for Pierre Bardinon. Cunningham's team colours of white with twin blue stripes adorned the Lightweight and its smooth-effect front.

This 1965 car is best described as a Semi-Lightweight. It was originally a left-hand-drive S1 4.2 roadster and was latterly reverse-engineered around 1990 by the Jaguar specialist Guy Broad using significant original E-Type Lightweight panels. The EOL 584C car was fitted with correct specification panels and driven by Sir Stirling Moss in competition. As such, this E-Type is unique in specification, build and use.

Vital original panels used in the rebuild of EOL 584C included the bonnet –which reputedly originating from the Ropner factory special-order Semi-Lightweight car that was a 1960s special of the type.

The correct, drilled and vented boot lid was fitted to EOL 584C and the hardtop was also accurate with its own vent panel and roof airflow ridge. Not one of the twelve 'pure' Lightweight' cars, it is an interesting and valid E-Type one-off nonetheless.

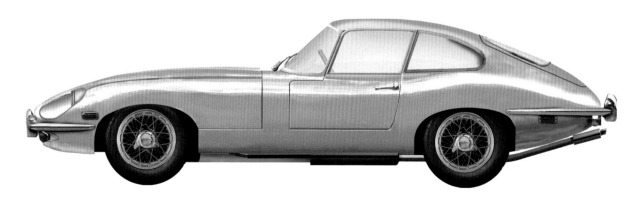

Many people preferred the fastback shape of the FHC-type design with its sleek and curved roof flowing back into a rakish tail. Depicted here in post-1967 S2 guise with un-faired headlamps and US-specification side repeater lamps, the original coupé design was elegant and distinctive. Despite the angled tail, Sayer reduced lift to as low as he could without resorting to a Kamm-type aerodynamic tail ridge or fence device.

The S2 cars retained E-Type's main body pressings but with minor changes. Of specific note was that the un-faired, vertical headlamps were of different setting and height within the front wing panel pressing, in comparison to the vertical, un-faired lamps fitted to the prior, limited production run S1.5 variation. Differences to the headlamp trim ring and wing beading were also of note.

The S2 featured revised front and rear lights and valances, larger bumpers and new badges. A host of interior improvements to seating, trims and specifications were also included. The rear tail hatch was side-opening.

With more room and more power via the silken 5343cc 24 valve V12, S3 was a different animal. Despite some styling changes, it still had real style and road presence. It was not 'ugly' by any means but lacked the early car's finesse: S3 in open or Roadster form weighed 3361lb/1527kg. Azure Blue, depicted here, was a 1970s Jaguar colour that was part of the change in image over earlier and more sober E-Type paint colours. Just 7,990 S3 Roadsters were built, with 7,297 Coupes made. An S3 Roaster cost £3,387 new in 1971.

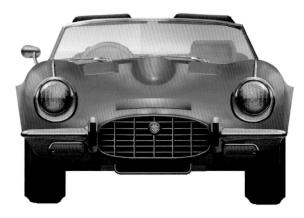 

The V12-engined S3 cars from 1971 had a longer wheelbase, and also wider wheel arches to accommodate larger wheels and tyres (pressed steel or optional wire). Of note, the S3 had a much larger front intake and a revised grille design with an under-valance air scoop. Two, not three, windscreen wipers were fitted to the new windscreen moulding. By late 1974, S3 was a victim of global fuel prices, age and corporate circumstance. The last fifty S3s were roadsters (forty-nine of which were black) yet offered with the newer steel hardtop roof design. By February 1975, E-Type S3 production was over.

Larger rear lamps (as first seen on the S2), revised exhaust, new badging and obviously larger bumpers marked the S3 out from the rear. The IRS with its driveshaft locaters, lower transverse links, anti-roll bar, radius arms, twin coil springs and dampers, was just about visible under that upswept tail. Jaguar used 'Metalastic' vibration-absorbing fixings in the rear suspension for the first time on E-Type and they later became a fitting on the 1968 Jaguar XJ saloon.

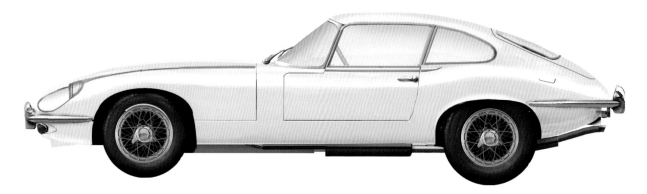

Utilizing the longer wheelbase 2+2 bodyshell introduced nearly four years earlier, the V12 S3 coupé, capable of 146mph, also used the longer body tub to offer some degree of rear seat accommodation. The longer wheelbase had also allowed fitment of an automatic gearbox and this continued to be offered. The roof profile was higher and the side window dimension different to the 'pure' original coupé design. Larger bumpers, new trims and US-specification kit detracted from the original design but E-Type assumed a new character and, with smooth V12 power, attacked a changing marketplace. Note the more curved, more raked new windscreen – finally smoothing out the airflow transition off the front to the side of the car with its cheap-to-produce flat glass side windows. Coupé production was set to end as the 1974 model year arrived at the end of the 1973 oil crisis.

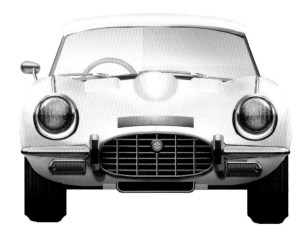

Wider, longer, larger, heavier, S3 also gained rubber over-riders in certain markets and had the flared wheel arches to accommodate wider wheels and tyres. New indicator lamps and new 1970s colours were added to the range.

Of note, the V12 S3 used the revised exhaust tailpipe design and a chromed extractor appliqué was added to the coupe's tail panel above the model badging. The new rear lamp valance taken from the S2 was less than elegant but at least the lamps were larger and brighter.

E- Type: well hued

The E-Type was originally available in up to twenty different colours. Thirteen interior trim/seat colour combinations were available. As S1, S2, and then the S3 model ranges evolved across 1961-1974 model years, a series of paint and trim colour deletes and additions were enacted. Up to 1972, Jaguar would paint a customer's new E-Type in any colour requested at extra cost. Special interior trim combinations were also offered in addition to factory specification palettes.

E-Type exterior paint colours by name:	Claret	Old English White	Black
Ascot Fawn	Cream	Pale Primrose Yellow	Blue
Beige	Fern Grey	Pearl	Cinnamon
Black	British Racing Green	Regency Red	French Blue
Blue	Opalescent Dark Green	Sable	Green
Lavender Blue	Sherwood Green	Signal Red	Grey
Azure Blue	Golden Sand	Silver	Light Green
Cotswold Blue	Greensand	Opalescent Silver Grey	Light Tan
Light Blue	Gunmetal	Turquoise	Maroon
Opalescent Light Blue	Heather	Warwick Green	Suede Grey
Dark Blue	Indigo	Wllow Green	Tan
Steel Blue	Imperial Maroon		Terracotta
Bronze	Opalescent Maroon	**Interior colours:**	
Carmen Red	Opalescent Grey	Beige	
	Mist Grey	Biscuit	

AMALGAM COLLECTION (BRISTOL, UK)
E-TYPE ROADSTER
1/8 SCALE

The claimed perfection of the 1/8 scale Amalgam Collection model of the E-Type across prototype reincarnation/continuation Project Zero E-Type and production models, is a big claim but one that is in fact delivered. This specific Amalgam Collection 1/8-scale E-Type opalescent blue roadster model is a limited-edition (199) model that has been handcrafted and finished with the co-operation and assistance of Jaguar regarding original finishes, materials, archive imagery and drawings. The use of digital scanning of an original car has allowed Amalgam to recreate every detail at accurate scale. It mimics not only the original, but also the recent continuation series from Jaguar in its perfection of form. Vital key points such as the scale and gauge of chrome trims, fixings, design details and the shapes and scaling of body contours

have been forensically rendered. The 1/8-scale E-Type from Amalgam is a lot of money but for the purist, a must-have. Amalgam also make E-Types at a slightly lower scale that retail at lesser prices which deliver a more egalitarian access point to what must be arguably the world's leading range of E-Type scale renditions. Of note, the model has undergone detailed scrutiny by both engineering and design teams to ensure complete accuracy. This Amalgam 1/8-scale model is mounted on a carbon-fibre or leather base protected by a clear acrylic dust cover. The model title, original branding and edition number are displayed on polished stainless-steel plaques mounted at the front end of the base. The Amalgam Collection also produce 1/18-scale Jaguar E-Type models in cast resin (with metal part fittings).

Is it real or it is scaled reality? The Amalgam Collection E-Type S1 roadster 1/8 scale justifies its price with superb scaling and detailing. Even the external bonnet catches are correct. A diecast resin build with metallic fittings applied in part, reflecting the first E-Type but also reflecting the Jaguar Classic continuation cars.

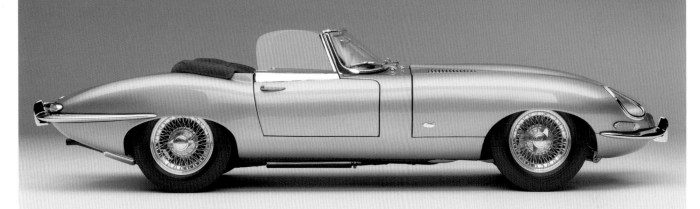

Front three-quarter view and the difficult-to-model headlamp surrounds and details of the wheels are clearly as near-perfect as a model can achieve. Only the windscreen wipers have presented a scaling challenge at 1/8.

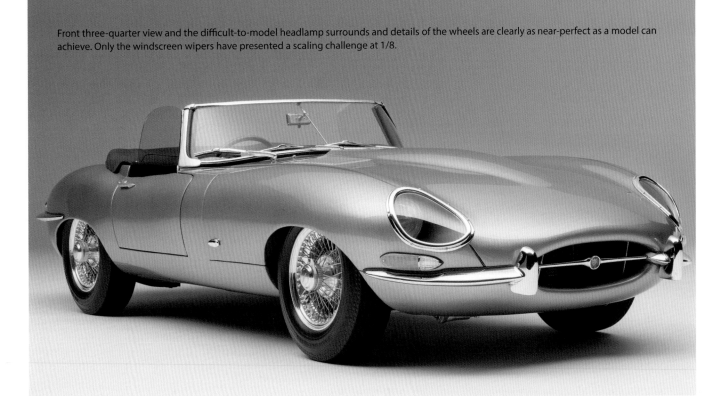

The front view shows off the accurate seams, panels, and even the rear-view mirror's scaling. From the rear, everything is accurate. The lack of a number registration plate being applied (due to customer demands) means that the number plate valance appears over-large, but it is not.

Seen from above, the lobed corners to the Sayer design are obvious – but E-Type is much squarer from this angle than others which makes more of its ellipsoid intent.

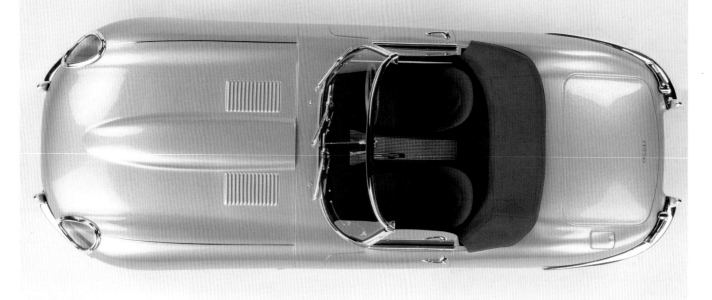

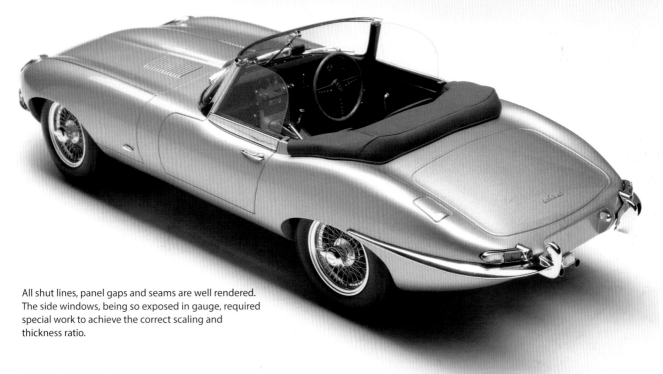

All shut lines, panel gaps and seams are well rendered. The side windows, being so exposed in gauge, required special work to achieve the correct scaling and thickness ratio.

From the door jambs and locks, the dashboard fittings, to the stowed fabric roof hood and the steering wheel, all is perfect. Only the scaling of the window-winder knob is debatable.

The open bonnet reveals the part-monocoque construction of the cabin body allied to the front spaceframe engine and system mountings. Note how the exhaust hangs correctly below the floorpan. This is the stuff of modelling forensics.

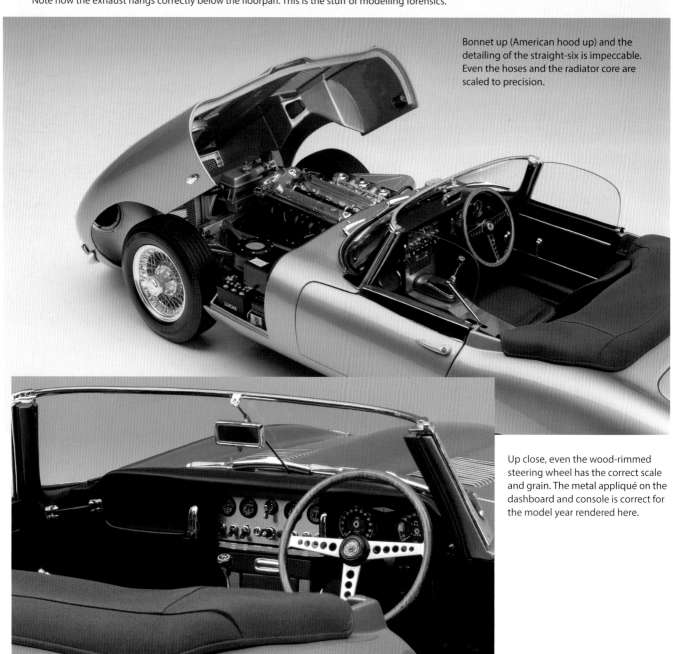

Bonnet up (American hood up) and the detailing of the straight-six is impeccable. Even the hoses and the radiator core are scaled to precision.

Up close, even the wood-rimmed steering wheel has the correct scale and grain. The metal appliqué on the dashboard and console is correct for the model year rendered here.

AMALGAM COLLECTION (BRISTOL, UK)
E-TYPE S1 COUPÉ
1/8 SCALE

The classic E-Type coupé in red at 1/8 scale. This is another of the Amalgam Collection and this time is the FHC fixed head with the fastback roof section and differing internal rear cabin area. Again, it has been handcrafted and finished with the co-operation and assistance of Jaguar regarding original finishes, materials, archive imagery and paint colour. The use of digital scanning of an original car has allowed Amalgam to recreate every detail within very fine ratios. Here the S1 coupé is seen in very early guise without door or wing mirrors and with external bonnet catches. Note also the standard, original wheelbase and the accurate modelling of the front and rear side windows (so often wrongly scaled in models). The wire wheels have also not been overdone. Created using expensive techniques, cast resin, metal fittings and many hundreds of hours of labour, this model is truly a wonderful tribute to the defining design and engineering of the E-Type. The red paint is correctly matched to the iconic Jaguar shade used from launch. A 199 limited-edition collector's piece, this is another expensive, but arguably unbeatable, effort from Amalgam – for the purist and well-heeled collector.

The superb accuracy of the details of the model are captured with the door open. Note also the excellent treatment to the rear side window, its trim, and the transition into the rear wing panel.

The perfect profile form of Malcolm Sayer's design shines though and shows why some people think it more of a cohesive sculpture than the roadster. The shape of the cabin turret and fastback seem to add to the E-Type's air of prehensile effect. The long bonnet can arguably have more visual dominance on the roadster design.

Coupé from the front with the difference in the windscreen header rails and roof panel obvious in comparison to the roadster. Coupé from the rear with the rear window detailing and roof profile correctly achieved in the body scaling. This model displays the original solo Jaguar script. The E-Type script was added by Jaguar at a later production date.

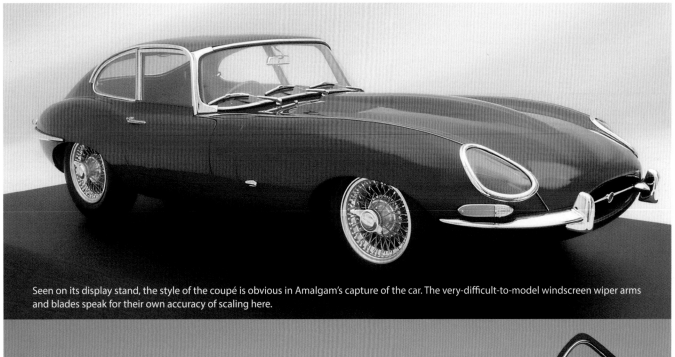

Seen on its display stand, the style of the coupé is obvious in Amalgam's capture of the car. The very-difficult-to-model windscreen wiper arms and blades speak for their own accuracy of scaling here.

Above: This view displays not just the clamshell bonnet (hood), but the rarely seen side-hinged rear tail door or hatch in action. The chrome window trims around the glazing are of highly accurate scale.

Left: The 3.8-litre XK engine captured in its element with every detail rendered. Note also the windscreen trim detail accuracy and bonnet pressing.

AUTOART
JAGUAR E-TYPE LIGHTWEIGHT
1/8 SCALE

AUTOart are rightly famous for their diecast E-Type range that extends to over a dozen versions. Here we see the stunning modelling of the Lightweight E-Type and a rare one in green fitted with racing roll cage and minus the more-expected fixed metal hardtop. This makes it all the more unusual. Superbly executed, the scaling is just right, the shut lines are good and the bodywork accurate. AUTOart produce the Lightweight in several liveries, the S1, S2 and S3 E-Types and in a range of carefully rendered and accurate period Jaguar paint schemes. Well priced from three- to four-figure levels (cited in GB pounds, US dollars and euros), this dedicated range of E-Types is rightly popular among enthusiasts, not least for the rarity value of some of the renditions alongside their technical accuracy.

Unusual in its green, this open-cockpit Lightweight with roll cage and accurate fittings shows what specialist effects can be achieved. The bonnet louvres are also well cast as are the Dunlop-type triple-winged wheel-hub nuts.

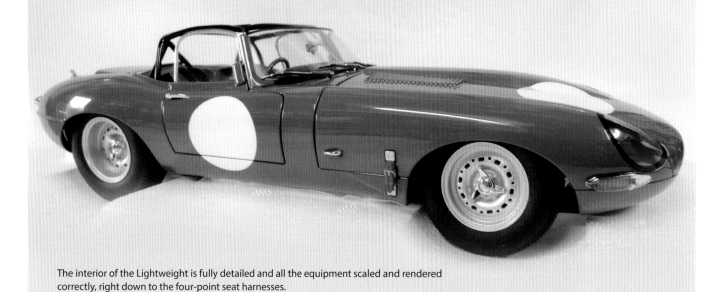

The interior of the Lightweight is fully detailed and all the equipment scaled and rendered correctly, right down to the four-point seat harnesses.

Wide-angle view on the rear end of the Lightweight shows off the drilled and vented boot lid and exhaust pipe details of AUTOart's presentation.

The sheer level of accuracy for the cost is a key AUTOart component. This close-up details the work that has gone into the rear lamp cluster and lenses. Stunning stuff.

For the price the AUTOart offering is strong. Here we see the leather bonnet strap, tyres, wheel wingnut and headlamp detail of the Lightweight type.

AUTOART
SERIES 1 E-TYPE 3.8 ROADSTER
1/18 SCALE

AUTOart seem to have done it again. Here we see modelled the classic S1 3.8-litre E-Type roadster in what some call Old English White. This model, one of a limited edition, truly captures the character of the roadster – with hood up/on or off. For the price bracket of this model, it offers some exceptional standards. Of particular note are the under-bonnet details and the cabin rendition. Given that the soft-top roof can be removed, exposing manufacturing standards in the cabin, can be a risk, but here AUTOart have pulled it off. The detailing of the headlamps, and notably the bumper 'blades', are top quality. Also visible is the front-end spaceframe construction and also the suspension design. Turning the model over reveals flat-floor-type construction and the expensive and complicated, Jaguar independent rear suspension. Such detailing provides the collector with a really worthwhile rendition of the classic E-Type.

The profile is perfect, the seams correct and even the inner front-wing flitch panel is accurate. The glazed and faired-in S1 headlamps look really good too. AUTOart seem to have really excelled with this one at reasonable price.

The rear end with every design detail correct. The E-Type's underbody was heavily upswept for aerodynamic reasons by its designer Malcom Sayer and this view portrays that feature. Note the chrome trim ring around number plate

Lift the roof off and reveal the cockpit/cabin in all its accuracy. Note the curious Jaguar handbrake lever – which in reality was not much use.

Accurate rear suspension with the IRS Salisbury-type diff and locater set-up design.

Front end forensics: so good is this detailing
that you might mistake it for the real thing.

Wire wheel and tyre shown in detail. This is superb modelling and scaling.

Above: XK engine under the bonnet with standard set-up and correct rocker covers.

Below: XK engine installation and triangulated spaceframe supports to provide mounting and alignment for all front-end components. These features were a D-Type derivation, captured here under the bonnet of the AUTOart achievement.

Modelling the E-Type

E-Type in Scale

Some classic car enthusiasts have little interest in model or scale renditions of their full-size cars. Yet perhaps of all cars (alongside the Porsche 911 and certain Bugatti and Ferrari cars), the E-Type has one of the strongest combined followings among modellers and E-Type owners alike. The Jaguar Enthusiasts' Club and the E-Type Club have dedicated model sections and regular coverage of model developments.Significantly, this global following focuses on metal die-cast models and resin die-cast models. The building of model kits of the E-Type does have a following, yet it is in the field of

pre-built, display-quality die-cast kits that a major E-Type market exists. Key scales of E-type modelling seem to be 1/144, 1/43, 1/32, 1/24 to 1/18, 1/13 and 1/8. Other scales and 1/200–1/500 also exist. From as early as 1963, Airfix launched an E-Type roadster as a plastic construction kit. Across the 1970s this was updated, retooled and re-boxed alongside a range of roadster and coupé models. Of note, it was at 1/32 scale that Airfix released their first E-Type kit in late 1963. In 1966 Airfix produced a motorized version. Airfix also sold an American-specification Jaguar XK-E as Airfix model code 2101 as early as 1967.

Cult Models' brilliant rendition of 4868WK, the Low Drag E-Type (the Lindner car) at 1/18 scale. Captured in accurate paintwork and scale, even the rivets are correct.

The revised roof, windscreen angle and side panels of the Low Drag car are all framed in this wonderful model.

The front of the Cult Models' Low Drag E-Type model shows superb detail work and highly realistic modelling of this unique car.

Seen from above, the very different tail design and roof canopy changes found amid the overall aerodynamic revisions carried out on the Low Drag E-Type are superbly captured in this model. Note rivet scaling and the accurate curved rear body shape.

This is detailing taken to new heights at 1/18 scale. The rear end is somehow even better. The Low Drag revised fastback roof shapes are all captured.

Close-up reveals the aerodynamic sculpting detail and the major changes to the back of the E-Type to control airflow, drag and lift.

MPC also released an American-nomenclature Jaguar XKE kit with the code of 7505 in 1969. Kits in various scales were soon to be released by major model making names such as Heller, Monogram, Revell, Frog and, of course, the revered Tamiya. Corgi, Vanguard and Dinky provided earlier models and, more recently, specialist model marques and distributors have turned to the E-Type. Heller's 1970s/1980s resin kit for modellers to build was at 1/24 scale and contained eighty-five parts to glue together to form an E-Type S1 coupé. Larger-scale kits and interesting specials such as the Low Drag and the Lightweight E-Types of Lindner, Cunningham and Coombs have featured in numerous releases; kit modellers still look to Tamiya for the brand's superb, expert detailing and forensic production standards when it comes to kit building the E-Type. Model forums such a Britmodeller and other web portals all feature superb E-Type kit-building discussions and build photos. In terms of the E-Type model popularity, it is the dominant die-cast market that supplies both E-Type body variations. These are well represented across the metal/hybrid metal, plastic/resin, diecast and vac-formed scale-model marketplace.

The side profile reveals the longer doors, higher roof and pulled-forward new windscreen shape.

White Box brand produced a 2+2 S2 with good body detailing but somewhat poorer wheel detail.

Non-faired headlamps captured in revised S2 2+2 E-Type by White Box.

The longer wheelbase and longer doors with higher roof did detract from the coupé's earlier styling, as seen on the White Box model.

AUTOart have released a large number of E-Type models (with prices ranging to four figures) and they have a strong following. Key scale is 1/18 and sees the S1 and S2 Series cars as the most prolific releases in a range of Jaguar colours. Roadsters and coupés are featured, notably with removable tops for the open cars, and excellent interiors. Paragon have turned out a range of dedicated E-Type Lightweight variants in liveries reflecting the car's 1960s motor-sport career. These are highly sought-after models. Shuco of Germany also produce a series of E-Types at more than one scale and as always with their output, quality is high; however, Shuco are also moving into the resin/metal hybrid construction arena. From the Amalgam Collection, via AUTOart, Paragon, Shuco and others, the E-Type remains a firm favourite. Yet newer names now appear large on the E-Type modelling landscape.

Above: Paragon perfection? The Briggs Cunningham (USA) E-Type Lightweight No. 2 car, its livery depicted in the Paragon version of the 1963 Le Mans racer: a real collectors' item.

Bottom page 60: The Cunningham car in correct form, with bubble hardtop fitted with a light. Note the louvres and addenda as they are all perfectly scaled.

IXO models, Premium X, Matrix, Oxford Diecast, Century Dragon and Best Models are all core names in E-Type modelling of one type or the other. These are the lead players in E-Type scale rendition. Burago have also produced both versions of the E-Type body in metal and despite some small issues relating to scales of trims and fittings, they are popular models in their sector.

Above and left: Premium X models marketed this rare model of the 1966 Raymond Loewy attempt to improve or restyle the E-Type for reasons best left undiscussed. This is the horrendous bling-style front grille he suggested.

Perhaps Loewy was trying to create a Toyota 2000GT, but the model is unusual so we include it here.

Century Dragon produced these two as a smaller-scale roadster and coupé pair. Although not perfect, they made an interesting die-cast display presentation at 1/43 scale.

The over-gauged side window trim strip detailing reveals the pitfalls of scaling and manufacturing in the mass market sector, but the model is not without merit.

However, it is the specialist die-cast model producers who now dominate the new and pre-owned die-cast kit market.

Cult Models, or Cult, are a brand with a strong list of Jaguar and E-Type models – mainly hand-crafted resin – right up to a recent XJR-15 release.

Matrix even captured the Perspex aerodynamic 'interference' fence that was placed on the bonnet to deflect debris and contamination away from the driver's vision side of the windscreen by vortex / pressure effect.

Left: A fitting tailpiece for an E-Type modelling section, the Lindner Low Drag car was an original Lightweight roadster converted to Low Drag fastback bodywork. Matrix made it work at smaller scale and Paragon models made it at 1/18 scale too.

Above left: Details of Cult's excellent S2 coupé rendition – note the accurate headlamp and trim ring portrayal and front-wing line and seam. The wheels look really good too.

Above right: Cult's fastback S2 in a darker red is a fantastic piece of work. The XKE number plate should appeal to American enthusiasts. Note the superb window trim detail and the perfect bumpers, lamps and badging.

Left: With attention to detail, the front quarter side of Cult's S2 coupé reveals just how good the wheels, tyres and bonnet louvres can be at this scale.

Below left: The Burago coupé captured the car's body shape.

Below right: Well priced and accessible, the Burago E-Type lacked scaling finesse and suffered from over-gauged fittings such as mirrors, catches and trims. However, a good entry kit for the larger-scale enthusiasts.

Burago produced two British Racing Green E-Types: one roadster and one coupé, both in the same colour and trim spec.

Key Modelling Points of E-Type

Whether building a kit, constructing a pre-part constructed self-build, or assessing a ready-built metal or resin die-cast model, several key ingredients are vital to accurate rendition of the E-Type:

Body contours.

Seams.

Panel gaps and shutlines.

Chrome trim detail and scaling.

Cabin turret and roof section shapes, scales and dimensions according to type.

Front headlamps and lights.

Rear lights.

Front intake grille shape and dimensions.

Bonnet catches.

Louvres.

Windscreen wipers.

Wheels – types and trims.

Glazing and chrome work.

External mirrors – type and positions according to year.

Seat types and interior specifications such as toggle switches/rocker switches and centre console finishes.

Engine details from rocker cover to carburation and spark plugs.

Rear exhaust pipe specifications and variations.

Tyres and wheel types.

Correct specifications to Series of car and model year and market variations.

Expert builders will seek to accurately render the various Low Drag, Lightweight and Semi-Lightweight E-Types and reference to accurate photographs are vital for such builds.

Left: Matrix produced this attractive gold 1970 model-year S2 roadster in a limited edition.

Below right: The Matrix S2 roadster was rather good, but let down by its over-thick windscreen frame. The tan interior looked good though.

Below left: Matrix made the folded roof hood look good and provided some acceptable casting for the price and the scale. These smaller modellers have found a niche in the enthusiast market.

Bottom: Matrix produced a smaller-scale variant of the Lindner Low Drag conversion car on chassis 850662. Although the Matrix model's rivets are a bit out of scale, the overall effect was successful and well received.

Acknowledgements/References:

Keith R. Powell Model Section, Jaguar Enthusiasts' Club; Jaguar Enthusiasts' Club magazine; Jaguar Cars Ltd.; Jaguar Classic; The Jaguar E-Type Club; The Amalgam Collection; Paragon Models; Chris and Bob at Froude and Hext Models; JDH Trust; *Classic Cars*, Bauer Media; *Octane*, D. Lillywhite, Dennis Publishing; *Jaguar: The History of a Great British Car*, Andrew Whyte for Jaguar Cars Edition/ Patrick Stephens Ltd.; *Jaguar E-Type: The Complete Story*, Jonathan Wood, Crowood Press; the late Michael Scarlett at *Autocar*; the late David Boole at Jaguar Cars; the late Innes Ireland; the late Blair Shenstone and family archives; the Sayer family; the *Daily Telegraph* archives; all friends at Jaguar and Jaguar clubs; Prescott Hill Climb; Bugatti Owners' Club facilities; dedicated to the life and works of Malcolm G. Sayer. All photos by Lance Cole, or Jaguar as cited.